Inclusive
Leadership

James Ryan

Inclusive
Leadership

JOSSEY-BASS
A Wiley Imprint
www.josseybass.com

Published by Jossey-Bass
A Wiley Imprint
989 Market Street, San Francisco, CA 94103-1741   www.josseybass.com

Jossey-Bass books and products are available through most bookstores. To contact Jossey-Bass directly call our Customer Care Department within the U.S. at 800-956-7739, outside the U.S. at 317-572-3986, or fax 317-572-4002.

Jossey-Bass also publishes its books in a variety of electronic formats. Some content that appears in print may not be available in electronic books.

Library of Congress Cataloging-in-Publication Data
Ryan, James, 1952 Oct. 18–
  Inclusive leadership / James Ryan.
    p. cm. — (Jossey-Bass leadership library in education)
  Includes bibliographical references and index.
  ISBN-13: 978-0-7879-6508-2 (alk. paper)
  ISBN-10: 0-7879-6508-1 (alk. paper)
    1. Educational leadership—United States. 2. School management and organization—United States. 3. Multiculturalism—United States. 4. Group decision making—United States. I. Title. II. Series.
  LB2801.A2R93 2006
  371.2'00973—dc22   2005012787

Printed in the United States of America
FIRST EDITION
PB Printing 10 9 8 7 6 5 4 3 2 1

THE JOSSEY-BASS
Leadership Library in Education

•

Andy Hargreaves
Consulting Editor

THE JOSSEY-BASS LEADERSHIP LIBRARY IN EDUCATION is a distinctive series of original, accessible, and concise books designed to address some of the most important challenges facing educational leaders. The authors are respected thinkers in the field who bring practical wisdom and fresh insight to emerging and enduring issues in educational leadership. Packed with significant research, rich examples, and cutting-edge ideas, these books will help both novice and veteran leaders understand their practice more deeply and make schools better places to learn and work.

ANDY HARGREAVES is the Thomas More Brennan Chair in Education in the Lynch School of Education at Boston College and the author of numerous books on culture, change, and leadership in education.

For current and forthcoming titles in the series, please see the last pages of this book.

Contents

The Author

James Ryan is a professor in the Department of Theory and Policy Studies at the Ontario Institute for Studies in Education, University of Toronto. He teaches courses in the educational administration program, including Theory in Educational Administration, Field Research in Educational Administration, Educational Leadership and Social Justice, and Educational Leadership and Cultural Diversity. Prior to entering academia, Ryan was a teacher and administrator in schools in northern Canada. His research interests—leadership, diversity, and inclusion—are reflected in his most recent research studies and publications, which include explorations of inclusion and leadership and of administrators' dialogue across differences. His most recent books are *Race and Ethnicity in Multiethnic Schools* and *Leading Diverse Schools*.

Inclusive
Leadership

The Case for Inclusive Leadership

Have you ever had a change of class or curriculum assignment without being consulted? Do waves of reform initiatives repeatedly disrupt your work, although you have had no say in how they are implemented, much less how they are designed? Does your district move you in and out of principalships with scarcely a thought for your wishes? If any of these things have happened to you, then you know what it's like to be excluded.

If you have been bullied or ostracized, teased or tormented because you were too fat or too skinny, too studious or too slow, you also know what it's like to be excluded. All of us have felt excluded at some time, and we know all too well the feelings of embarrassment and humiliation that can result. But for some people, exclusion happens every day, repeatedly and systematically. As well as hurting their feelings, it destroys their opportunities and ruins their lives, especially if they are denied educational opportunities and the basic right to learn.

If you are forbidden to speak and learn in your own language, if the content of the curriculum and of standardized tests favors other people's cultures more than yours, if your parents are labeled as lazy because they cannot leave their night jobs to get to meetings at the school, or if teachers have only low expectations for you because you are black or female or poor, then the educational exclusion you experience cuts to the core of your life and your opportunities within it.

For all the current talk of instructional leadership, transformational leadership, or even distributed leadership or of closing achievement gaps between the advantaged and the rest, the theory and practice of educational leadership have little to say about these pernicious and pervasive processes of exclusion. They set out no coherent vision of what leadership that promotes its opposite—inclusion—would look like. This book tries to fill this gap by laying out a vision of inclusive leadership.

We need to look on leadership as a collective influence process that promotes inclusion. Such leadership is inclusive in two ways. First, the process itself is inclusive; it includes as many individuals and groups and as many values and perspectives as possible in decision-making and policymaking activities. Second, inclusive leadership promotes inclusive practices. Inclusive leadership is organized above all to work for inclusion, social justice, and democracy not just in school and local communities but also in wider national and global communities. This book makes a case for inclusive leadership, sketching out the dimensions of exclusion, analyzing the research on inclusive leadership, and setting out a framework for putting inclusive leadership into practice.

Beacon Elementary School

Beacon Elementary is one of a small but growing number of schools that employ inclusive leadership.[1] Beacon is unique in ways other than its inclusive practices. One of the most obvious is that it is not yet housed in a normal school building. With the exception of some kindergarten and first-grade classes that are held at the neighboring school, the school population—from kindergarten to fifth grade—occupies a platoon of sixteen small portable structures. Arranged in three neat but uneven rows and nestled beside Beacon's sister school, these little brown buildings are home to almost eight hundred students. The neighboring school, dwarfed in population but not in physical size by Beacon, is a handsome, low-slung brick building that meshes nicely with the smallish but comfortable bungalows that dominate the surrounding residential area. This community, however, is not the one that Beacon serves. Beacon's catchment area is a good mile-and-a-half or twenty-minute drive away, located in the midst of a rapidly growing urban sprawl. Students, teachers, and parents are all looking forward to the time when the school can move from the portables into a new building.

Beacon's student population is diverse. Twenty years ago, this would have been unique. Today, Beacon's population is not much different from most other schools in the area. Changing immigration and settlement patterns have generated many communities of the sort that Beacon serves. Students or their parents come from all over the world. Many identify with countries like Jamaica, Guyana, India, and China; there are few white faces among them. But while this diversity may not be unique, the way in which the school approaches diversity is. Beacon endeavors to find ways to include all members of the school community in its activities. It is committed to including its community—teachers, parents, and students—not only in decision-making processes but in the activities of the school generally. This is no small task, given the significant obstacles, not the least of which is the school's physical layout.

Beacon Elementary School values inclusion and thus attempts to include all members of the school community and their values, knowledge, and culture in the day-to-day activities of the school. The value of inclusion is reflected in the symbols that the school uses and in the activities that it sponsors. Beacon has two symbols that reflect how it values inclusion. The first is their school animal— a Bengal tiger. Voted in by students, it also symbolizes a country with which many of the students identify: India. The other symbol is the school colors. Beacon has not one but many colors: those of the rainbow. These are displayed around the school in such artifacts as flags. Not by coincidence, the rainbow flag is also the gay pride flag. All the teachers are aware of this, and it is not an issue. Of course, inclusion goes beyond these symbols. Inclusion is part of Beacon's attempts to promote a culture of safety and affection; the manner in which it involves students, parents, and teachers and their values and knowledge in the school's activities; and the way it confronts exclusive processes like racism.

At Beacon, inclusion goes hand in hand with shaping a culture of affection and safety. Joanne, the principal, says that the school wants "to build a culture of affection":

> Children see staff being affectionate and respecting everyone regardless of who your grandparents are or what language they speak. And they see us being silly, dressing up, and it makes children feel comfortable. If you are uncomfortable being silly, this isn't the place for you. It's not just school spirit, it's the whole issue of feeling safe. The phrase *safe schools* is usually used when you are talking about bullies, but it is far more than that. The school is a haven; it is not just a place for academics. If a kid doesn't feel safe at school, forget the academics. You don't have a chance. First, a child has to feel safe and loved; then they will learn.[2]

Joanne also believes that security and affection cannot be achieved with individual acts or isolated programs but must be embodied in everything the school does. The priority of providing security and affection, already embedded in the burgeoning school culture, involves a whole-school effort. It finds expression, for example, in the school rules. Developed collectively and referred to as Beacon Promises, these regulations are written in language that students can understand, and they apply to everyone, not just students. The first and most important of the Beacon Promises states, "I promise to treat others as I would like to be treated."

Beacon includes teachers in the school's decision-making processes. They have ownership of school activities such as staff meetings. Teachers chair these gatherings, determine the agenda, and decide on the issues. They also control the budget, set the calendar, and determine the need for and the membership of committees. The case of the English as a Second Language reception planned for next year typifies this process. After recognizing the need for this sort of activity, teachers formed a committee to look into the issue. In the next few weeks, the committee met, came up with alternatives, and brought them to a staff meeting in which teachers came to a consensus on a plan. Joanne feels this ownership is crucial. She has seen too many schools that have been driven by the personality of the principal. In these situations, many of the school's values and practices leave when the principal does. To avoid such a scenario, Joanne and Beacon's vice principal, John, support a structure for teachers that enables them to do things on their own. She believes that this structure will survive their tenure at the school and provide the basis for future inclusion. Joanne is confident that Beacon will not have to begin again when a new principal arrives.

Beacon includes the community in its activities. It reaches out to parents by involving them in decision making, communicating with them, and endeavoring to make them feel comfortable. Parents are involved in the activities of the school through a school council. In order to be as inclusive as possible, the council has agreed to let everyone who wishes share in chairing the council. Currently, it has three parent chairs; they are referred to affectionately as "co-co-chairs." The school also actively works at communicating with parents. One of its most effective tools is the newsletter, which asks many questions of parents—for example, whether and how they want to become involved in fundraising, what kind of after-school activities they would prefer for students, and which teachers they want for their children in the upcoming year. The school also works hard at making parents feel comfortable when they visit the school. This is perhaps best reflected in the approach that Joanne and John take. They project an unpretentious image, introducing themselves by their first name, saying little of their background, and leaving out testaments to their past accomplishments. Joanne physically touches people, and she holds their babies, hoping to convey the impression that they are in a day camp rather than a formal institution. One of the things that puts immigrant parents at ease when they come in for the first time is identifying their former home. The school has acquired a detailed map of India, and administrator, parent, and child are usually able to identify the precise community where an Indian parent or child has roots. Finally, Beacon has a number of teachers of Punjabi and West Indian heritage who can converse with parents about issues of concern in English, Punjabi, Urdu, or Hindi.

Beacon tries to ensure that all students are meaningfully included in its learning processes and other activities. It provides them with opportunities to influence what happens in the school and to identify with the things about which they learn. The school uses the newsletter to survey student wishes. In the past, students have influenced the name of the school mascot, issues involving a dance-a-thon, and various fundraising activities. Apart from these chances to influence decisions, fourth- and fifth-grade students have opportunities to be bus monitors, kindergarten helpers, and peace pals—students who help other students get along with one another. The school also has a Punjabi report card, uses dual-language books, and attempts to include students' cultural experiences in the curriculum and school activities as much as possible. In addition, Beacon staff work hard at pronouncing student names; none are Anglicized.

Beacon actively confronts sensitive issues like race and racism. It does not take for granted or gloss over the fact that everyone in the school community is "raced" or pretend that racism does not exist at the school. Instead, teachers and staff encourage conversations about issues associated with race, culture, and religion. They also educate the school community in these matters and take action when there is evidence of racist behavior. In one instance, a second-grade student told a boy that she couldn't play with him because he was black. After a conversation with the girl and her father, Joanne suspended the student. She felt that a message had to be sent so that norms could be established. Joanne wanted to let the community know that neither students nor anyone else are permitted to hurt others' feelings because of an area of life over which they have no control. She maintained that while people are allowed to dislike others if the others "are jerks," people are not allowed to make others feel bad about their race, religion, language, place of birth, ability, or other such characteristics.

Beacon Elementary School is committed to inclusion and inclusive leadership. It understands the deep-seated nature of exclusion and has begun to embed inclusion in its governance and learning processes. This is no small achievement. To do this, it has had to overcome many significant obstacles in both the immediate and the wider environment. To begin with, Beacon is in its infancy. As a new school, it has just begun to develop its own culture and has yet to call a conventional building "home." Nonetheless, despite significant impediments, Beacon has persevered through its first year, making its fledgling school community an inclusive and welcoming place. This significant accomplishment has only been attained through the compassion, courage, and commitment of students, educators, and parents.

The members of Beacon's school community have consistently demonstrated their compassion and caring. They have forged a culture of affection and safety because they believe that it is important for children to feel loved and secure. Joanne maintains that this task comes before academics; students learn best when they feel safe and cared for. Toward this end, educators have made the school a welcoming haven by modeling affection, acting silly at times, avoiding professional pretentiousness, and, above all, by following and enforcing their number one school rule—treating others as they would like to be treated themselves. Beacon has also demonstrated its compassion by valuing the knowledge, culture, and language of all students and parents. As far as possible, it includes these in the curriculum, in teaching and learning, and in other activities.

Beacon's students, educators, and parents have shown their courage in a number of ways. Joanne and John have led the way. It has not been easy for them to withdraw from many of the decision-making processes and to trust others to act on issues for which they are responsible. But they have done it, and the entire school community is the better for it. Joanne, John, and the rest of the staff have also risked conflict and criticism by stripping away their protective professional images and making a point of confronting difficult issues like racism. The risk has been worthwhile, for these measures have engendered a welcoming and secure space for students and parents. Parents have also shown their courage by supporting the school on these issues and stepping forward to make themselves heard in what can be an uncertain, alien, and threatening environment.

The Beacon community is committed to inclusion. Students, educators, and parents are determined to carry through with their inclusive philosophy. Joanne and John have taken steps to support the school community in this quest by putting structures in place that will make it comfortable to commit to inclusion and that will ensure that these practices will survive their tenure. But Beacon is just in its infancy. Only time will tell how this commitment will endure. Beacon still has much to learn from both schools that have failed and schools that have passed the test of time and change.[3]

Obstacles to Inclusion

Beacon is representative of a growing number of school communities, school districts, and government agencies that are committed to inclusion. They are to be applauded for wanting to see, as recent U.S. legislation does, that no child gets left behind.[4] This is a worthy goal. It acknowledges, quite rightly, that not all students are able to succeed in school and that this situation needs to be corrected. Too many young people do not experience schooling in ways that allow them to thrive. One of the reasons for this is that they are not included in ways that provide them with the best learning experiences. In other words, they are excluded. And exclusion can be painful.

All of us have been excluded at one time or another. We may have been excluded by not being asked out as adolescents or by not being regarded as cool because we were overweight, shy, or studious. We may have been excluded when we were newcomers to a school or a neighborhood and people talked about us among themselves. People are excluded when they are bullied or silenced or ignored. These kinds of exclusions can arise as the result of personal cruelty or, often, mere thoughtlessness. Some feelings of exclusion may be inevitable when you join a new group, team, or culture; they represent a stage in the process of becoming a full-fledged member. But being excluded is not a pleasant thing to experience. We feel shame, hurt, and embarrassment. So imagine what it must feel like when exclusion is repeated time and again, when it is systematic, when your ethnicity, skin color, gender, sexual orientation, financial position, or body shape result in you being excluded over and over.

Exclusion occurs regularly both in school and in the wider community. Too many are excluded from the key learning processes, and they suffer the consequences, both as young people and as adults. But in a democratic society or, for that matter, any society, humanity has an obligation to see that everyone is included fairly not just in schooling processes but in all social, cultural, economic, and political institutions. Everyone has the right to participate in what the world has to offer and to reap the benefits of this involvement. Regrettably, at this time, this is not happening.

Children continue to be excluded from what their schools and society have to offer for a number of reasons. One, of course, is a reluctance to acknowledge and confront exclusion. Exclusion has deep roots, and if it is not challenged, it will persist. But another significant cause of exclusion is the failure of those who support inclusion to recognize the extent of exclusion. While advocates may concede that not all children do well in schools, some cannot understand or will not admit that this exclusion is part of deeply entrenched and often subtle patterns in schools and communities. They refuse to admit that exclusion is intimately associated with practices of racism, sexism, classism, homophobia, and ableism or that these patterns continue to be part of the fabric of everyday school and community life, including some accepted practices of learning. Exclusion can, for example, find expression in testing arrangements. This is one of the problems with the No Child Left Behind Act.[5] Despite its surface concern with marginalized students, it continues to exclude already marginalized students through the testing schemes it favors. By ignoring local knowledge and culture, this testing systematically devalues what many students bring to school and makes it difficult for teachers to design lessons that complement these attributes.

There is plenty of evidence that illustrates how these tests are exclusive. Linda McNeil has provided compelling evidence from a study she carried out in Texas that shows how such testing penalizes students who are already marginalized by virtue of race, class, and culture relationships.[6] Other, more graphic examples also make the point. I know of a case in which one young woman was frustrated by the content of a question on one of these tests. Although Mary immigrated to Canada many years ago from a non-European country, she gets along quite nicely in the English language. Despite her comfort with English, Mary had difficulty with a question that was based on the tradition of scouting. She did not know enough about it to understand the question or what was expected for an answer. This is not surprising, given that scouting is part of a British tradition with which Mary is not familiar. She had not been brought up with or exposed to this tradition and, as a consequence, was not in a position to answer the questions on the test that required knowledge of it. Even so, she and many other students from non-

Western backgrounds were expected to answer the questions in the same way as those who were familiar with scouting traditions.

If we are serious about inclusion in our schools and communities, then we must acknowledge these deeply entrenched and often taken-for-granted patterns of exclusion and commit to doing something about them. The first step in this process is for school communities to adopt inclusive leadership practices. Like the administrators at Beacon Elementary School, educators must include the whole school community in influence processes. In these sorts of arrangements, everyone has the opportunity to have their voice heard in governance and decision-making processes. For this to endure, participation needs to be embedded in structures that transcend the influence of particular individuals. Leadership practices also have to be guided by an inclusive philosophy; they need to be organized to promote inclusive processes generally, moving beyond decision-making and policymaking processes to a concern with wider issues of inclusion. Only in this way will schools and communities be able to build institutions that are truly inclusive.

But Beacon and other schools that are interested in promoting inclusion also face many other more global obstacles—for example, the entrenched hierarchical structure of education systems, skepticism about inclusive and participative leadership, existing perceptions about leadership, and the difficulty of linking leadership processes to wider practices of inclusion.

While many people express their support for inclusive forms of leadership, they do not always follow through with it in practice. Many things prevent inclusion. One of the biggest hurdles is the hierarchical structure of education systems, in which responsibility for everything that goes on inside (and sometimes outside) school buildings rests solely with principals. Principals may be responsible not only for such basic concerns as schedules, budgets, and student safety but also for many other more trivial matters, such as ensuring that the drink machine in the cafeteria is working. Principals bear the brunt of the blame when things go wrong, so it is not always easy for them to trust others to participate or make decisions in areas for which they, as principals, are solely responsible.

Recent management approaches have reinforced this hierarchy. The new managerial trend in schools, for example, emphasizes the distinction between managers and policymakers, and everyone else who works in organizations.[7] Initially conceived as a response to declining revenues for public education, resistance on the part of educators to current school practices and policies, and the unfounded perception that educators are to blame for the problems with schools, this management-oriented approach to leadership endorses the principle that some people need to make decisions for others because they are more capable. Policymakers and senior administrators are encouraged to formulate policies that limit the often unreliable actions of lower-echelon administrators and teachers, who, in turn, are trusted to execute policies but not to design, interpret, or question them. For their own and students' good, they are merely to put these policies into practice. This new managerialism is reflected in recent reform initiatives that favor standardized testing and teacher-proof curriculum, practices that prohibit teachers from using their expertise when testing and teaching and that prevent the community from having any input.

These kinds of externally mandated reforms can seriously challenge inclusive practice in schools. Take the case of Blue Mountain School.[8] Widely recognized as an innovative school since its inception in 1994, it is now straining to maintain its unique orientation under the weight of centralized reforms that feature centralized, subject-based curriculum and testing. Corrie Giles and Andy Hargreaves show how these edicts have chipped away at all aspects of Blue Mountain's work and culture, deflecting it away from its global learner philosophy, overloading teachers with work, undermining opportunities for teachers to learn together, and ultimately undercutting the commitment to its vision. A teacher at the school comments on how these reforms have changed the way in which inclusion works in their planning: "We (used to) meet to decide as a group how best to go about a process. Well there's been no meeting. We've just been told these classes are closed. And never in my whole career has that ever happened. There isn't that opportunity to share information. And now it's just sort of 'top down' because there's only time for top down."[9]

This entrenched hierarchy has given rise to skepticism about whether efforts to include everyone in decision-making processes will change anything.[10] Some say that such efforts will waste people's time, delay important decisions, raise operating costs, and increase workloads. But if hierarchies remain, efforts at inclusion will also be fake, just another subtle way to extend control over the actions of local educators by diffusing conflict throughout the system, creating a buffer between local educators and government, and deflecting criticism away from the government. Critics also say that those who are traditionally excluded from leadership processes will continue to be left out of current initiatives; the nature of these superficial inclusive arrangements will make it difficult, if not impossible, for those on the margins to become meaningfully involved in them, and the power relationships, technical language, and collusion of educators and middle-class parents will make it difficult for inclusion to be full or fair.[11]

Another serious obstacle to inclusive practice is the way that people perceive leadership in terms of positions or individuals who act in certain exclusive ways.[12] Many continue to accept the principle that leadership is embodied in particular individuals. Because advocates believe that these men and women have within themselves the capacity to influence others, they look to them to do great things, particularly in times of uncertainty and turmoil. Gandhi, Churchill, and De Gaulle are frequently cited as exemplars that current leaders ought to emulate.[13] But it is unrealistic to expect such feats from most individuals. Research by Philip Hallinger and Ronald Heck illustrates that individual principals have only a "relatively small" influence on schools.[14] It is likely that groups of people working together will have greater influence on what happens in schools than a single individual.[15] The individualistic view of leadership precludes perspectives that see it as a more inclusive, collective process.

Another impediment to inclusive leadership is the difficulty of linking participation in decision-making processes to the ends for which these processes are organized. Many of the current inclusive approaches to leadership do not extend much beyond school leadership processes themselves. Many teacher leadership approaches, for example, focus on efforts to include teachers in decision-making processes but ignore more global commitments to inclusion. Indeed, many of those who favor teacher participation in decision-making processes increasingly do so for pragmatic rather than moral reasons.[16] They favor including teachers in decision-making processes because they believe that it will help principals do their job and increase student achievement.[17]

To ensure inclusion, leadership approaches must emphasize both the process and the product. If leadership is to be truly inclusive, it must promote the ideals of inclusion, democracy, and social justice more generally. Not only must inclusive school leadership processes practice inclusion, but they must also advocate for it in their schools, communities, and the world as part of a far-reaching pursuit of inclusion, democracy, and social justice across schools and communities. As well as being broad, truly inclusive leadership in education needs to run deep, ensuring that all members of the school community and their perspectives are included fairly in all school processes, especially in learning processes.

Designing, implementing, and sustaining inclusive leadership practices in schools will be a formidable challenge. This is not to say, however, that such a goal is unattainable. On the contrary, it has been successfully met in a small but significant number of schools, including Beacon Elementary School. But Beacon's version of inclusive leadership is just one of many. In the next two sections, I clarify the concepts of inclusion and inclusive leadership.

Inclusion

Recently, many of those concerned with seeing that all people enjoy the same kinds of opportunities in life and in school have begun using the term *inclusion*.[18] On the surface, the term *inclusion* and its more familiar root word, *include*, are reasonably straightforward. *Include* means to enclose, to be part of a whole, to contain, or to take into account.[19] When the concept of inclusion is applied in social situations, however, things become a little more complicated. One way to think about inclusion in social situations is to consider the type of access people get to societal systems. To what extent do men, women, and children have access to social, economic, political, or cultural systems—to participation in decision-making and political processes, to employment and material resources, and to common cultural processes like education?[20] Not everyone has the opportunity to be part of these systems in the same manner, and those who do not generally do not experience the same quality of life as those who do. This is not right or fair. Everyone should have the right to be part of these practices and to share the opportunities and rewards that accompany them. This book is based on the assumption that everyone deserves to be included fairly in all systems and practices of school and society.

The idea and practice of inclusion has been part of education for some time now, but it has typically been associated only with the education of "special needs," "exceptional," or "differently abled" students.[21] Inclusion has been presented as a strategy that is designed to counteract the common practice of removing these students from mainstream, or "regular," classes. Advocates of inclusion sought to ensure that differently abled students would attend classes with other types of students instead of being separated. Based on the "belief that all children with disabilities have a right to be educated alongside nondisabled peers," inclusive education of this sort "attempts to bring all students, including those with disabilities, into full membership with their local school community."[22]

More recently, the concept of inclusion in education has been expanded to address not just differently abled students but everyone in the school community. Others besides differently abled students are excluded from important school activities. Students have different levels of access to schools, and some do not even attend school at all. Students may also find themselves routinely excluded from the knowledge, experiences, and interactions that schools favor, even when they are physically present.[23] Even in common classrooms, students may find that they do not or cannot identify with what teachers teach, with the social interactions that prevail, or with the experiences that result. Regrettably, this exclusion prevents them from getting the most out of their schooling experience. So if educators want to see that all students have the best possible educational experiences, they are obliged to do their utmost to ensure that all students are allowed to be included in everything they have to offer. This requires educators to discover or invent routines to affirm the different knowledge, experiences, cultures, and histories of the students who attend their schools.[24]

Student inclusion in learning processes is, of course, an important part of inclusive practice. But leadership is also a critical element.

Inclusive Leadership

The view of leadership that I endorse here may not sit well with everyone. One of my graduate assistants does not even recognize it as a type of leadership at all. An astute student of leadership himself, he favors a more conventional view that acknowledges that there are people who lead and people who follow.[25] In contrast, I see *inclusive leadership* not in terms of positions or individuals who perform certain tasks but as a collective process in which everyone is included or fairly represented.

What do I mean by *leadership?* In the broadest sense, I think of it as a collective process of social influence that is aimed at a particular end.[26] This definition has three key elements. First, leadership implies some sort of *influence*. People exert influence and are influenced in turn. This influence may be obvious—for example, when certain individuals overtly affect the outcome of a decision—or it may be subtle—for example, when people seem to be able to surreptitiously sway what happens or when taken-for-granted forces work through them.[27] Influence occurs within leadership activities and as a result of them. Individuals or groups may vie to have their views reflected in decisions or policies. In addition, the outcomes of leadership deliberations or actions may have an impact on what happens in the school or wider community. Ideally, inclusive leadership provides everyone with a fair chance to influence decisions, practices, and policies. Advocates of inclusive leadership also trust that their deliberations will influence what happens in the school community and beyond.

Second, inclusive leadership is a *process*, an array of practices, procedures, understandings, and values that persist over time. Inclusive leadership does not associate leadership with dominant or central individuals who are expected to do great things by virtue of their personalities, their skills, or the positions they hold. Instead, inclusive leadership relies on many different individuals who contribute in their own often humble ways to a clearly established process. In this view, an individual may be a key mover in one situation and an observer in another. This means that the process will be able to withstand the departure of any individual or group of individuals. Inclusive leadership, then, is a collective process in which many people work together in a variety of ways to make things happen.

Third, inclusive leadership is organized to achieve particular *ends*. Some views of leadership prefer to emphasize the influence-generating or process side of leadership and ignore the particular values that it promotes. In such descriptions, even despots might be considered noteworthy leaders because they are able to achieve the goals that they favor, regardless of what these goals may be.[28] Inclusive leadership, however, promotes a very definitive end: inclusion.

It is not just the process of leadership that is inclusive; the ends of the process are also geared toward inclusion. Inclusive leadership aims to achieve inclusion in all aspects of schooling and beyond the school to the local and global community, and it does so through a process that is itself inclusive.

The remainder of this book explores and advocates for the idea, ideal, and practice of inclusive leadership. It gives a sense of the problems associated with inclusion and exclusion, a review of the research that has been done on inclusive leadership, and some practical suggestions for promoting and practicing inclusive leadership. Chapter Two elaborates on what exclusion is, how it shows up in schools, and how it affects individuals and institutions. That chapter also describes three other popular views of leadership and illustrates how they are actually exclusive. Chapter Three reviews the research on inclusive leadership. Finally, Chapter Four provides readers with a practical and flexible framework for practicing and promoting inclusion and inclusive leadership. Ultimately, I hope that this book will provide readers with enough information and inspiration about inclusive leadership that they, like Joanne, John, and the other members of the Beacon Elementary community, will find the compassion, courage, and commitment to pursue it successfully in their own settings.

2

The Problem of Exclusion

I nclusion's alter ego is exclusion. They are intimately related, for when people are not included, they are excluded. The task, then, is to include them. Inclusion is a problem today because of the existence of widespread forms of exclusion. Not only are people excluded from school leadership activities, but they are also left out of many other activities and privileges in school and in the local and wider communities in which they live and work. This is not right. Everyone should have the right to be included fairly in all community and school practices and activities.

This chapter focuses on two key areas of exclusion in schools and elsewhere. First, in schools and in the wider community, people who belong to certain groups suffer exclusion more than those who do not. Poor people, those associated with non-Western heritages, women and girls, and gay people routinely experience exclusion more than other people. These sorts of exclusion continue to evolve in new and obstructive ways. They occur in the new patterns in which work is organized, in recent responses to diversity initiatives, and in complacency about perceived progress in eliminating discrimination on the basis of gender and sexual orientation. These kinds of exclusion are serious problems to be acknowledged, addressed, and eliminated. They are also problems for educators because they invariably find their way into schools. Second, many popular approaches to leadership are also exclusionary, even though that may not be their intent. This chapter explores these two aspects of exclusion—exclusion in schools and society and exclusion in leadership theory.

Exclusion

Like its antonym, *inclusion,* the term *exclusion* appears to be reasonably straightforward. *Exclude* means to refuse to admit, consider, include; keep from entering, happening, or being; reject; bar; put out; force out; expel; or banish.[1] Just like *inclusion,* however, when the term *exclusion* is applied to social situations and to schools, it becomes more complicated. In the case of schools, exclusion encompasses both the more apparent physical aspects and the more shadowy social ones. Students are excluded when they are physically absent but also when they have difficulty in gaining entry to a school's various activities, experiences, and knowledge even when they are physically present. Let us look at exclusion in action.

Peter MacDonald School[2] sits prominently atop a rise that overlooks a vast expanse of water, a set of distant mountains that, with the first snowfall, look as if you could reach out and touch them, and the Native community that it serves. The contrast with the community is stark. The massive school building dwarfs the rows of tiny wood-frame houses that dot the hillside. The community itself has a relatively short history. Established in the early 1960s, it is home to the Innu, a nomadic First Nation people. The people had little choice but to settle here at the time. Faced with dramatic decreases in game animals that they depended on for survival, the difficulty of conducting their hunting activities under government-imposed restrictions, and pressures from church and state, the Innu abandoned their nomadic life to live year-round in this community.[3] The transition has not been easy; many social problems have resulted. Formal schooling, however, has been with them in one form or another from the beginning. In the community's early years, the local priest conducted lessons in makeshift settings. In time, the current school was built, integrated into the provincial school system, and populated by teachers from outside the Innu community.

The period in the school's history that I will describe is the mid-1980s, when the school's exclusive practices were most transparent. Since that time, the school has moved on; its current practices are decidedly more inclusive.[4] The exclusion of the community from the school during those earlier years was perhaps best symbolized by a sign posted by the principal. Tacked to the main door of the school and written in the Native language, it instructed potential visitors that they would not be welcome in the school unless they first checked in at the office. Apparently, the principal wanted to avoid potential disruptions of classes by parents and community members and supposed the sign would do the trick. The irony was that community members rarely, if ever, approached or entered the school during operating hours. If they did show up on school grounds, the last thing they would have felt comfortable doing would be presenting themselves at the office for inspection. Although this practice might be appropriate in an urban area, many community members believed it was not called for in a small community in which everyone knew one another. The message they took from the sign was that parents were not welcome at the school. This was just one way in which they were excluded, however. The community and students were excluded from other school practices. They were physically excluded by the school's schedule; excluded in other ways by the curriculum and the patterns of interaction favored by teachers; and excluded from decision making and policy deliberations.

MacDonald's schedule excluded students from its activities. Like other schools in the government system, MacDonald adopted a traditional seasonal schedule. The school year ran from September to June, with the usual holiday times in winter and spring. While this schedule was suitable for most communities and for the teachers who taught at the school, it did not coincide with traditional Innu activities. Many Innu continued to follow their seasonal hunting patterns even after they had taken up residence in the community. Each fall, many families would leave the community to go into the bush to hunt until Christmas, and their children would miss school at this time. It was not uncommon for over half the children in some classes to be absent. Despite this migration, the school did nothing to adjust its schedule or to compensate for the missed time. So students who missed classes—especially the many who missed school at this time every year—would fall further and further behind.

MacDonald's curriculum excluded community knowledge and experience. The school's official curriculum was "Canadian." As a school in the provincial system, it employed curriculum guidelines, textbooks, and other materials that most other schools in the district and the province used. While it did make efforts to include the Native language in the primary grades and provide a course on some aspects of Innu culture, the modifications did not amount to much. Students had to attempt to identify with experiences and accounts in textbooks that had little to do with their own experiences and community. One day, a young man involved in local politics came to the school and complained to the principal about one of the geography texts. This text, like most of the others that students used that covered the geography of Canada, described in detail the border between the provinces of Quebec and Newfoundland and Labrador. The man pointed out that the Innu do not acknowledge this border. For them, Innu land—which they call Netissinan—extends from Labrador well into Quebec. Their belief is that this land has been theirs to live and hunt in from time immemorial and that no borders cut across it. The principal listened to the young man's explanation and protests, but in the end declined to accept his argument. He took no steps to include the Innu version in geography classes or to change or drop the text.

The style of interacting and communicating at MacDonald also excluded students and community members from participating fully in school and classroom activities. Except in the primary grades, the language of instruction was English, a second language for all community members. Some people spoke English, but many of those spoke it poorly. The same was true for students; many could get by in conversation, but it was evident that just as many had serious difficulties with communicating in English. This language barrier was significant because the common style of teaching in the school emphasized talking and writing rather than visually demonstrating, as is common in many Native settings.[5] Language difficulties were compounded in the classroom by instructional styles that prominently featured student demonstrations of their knowledge. Getting up in front of others and addressing them was something that children did not do in their homes or in the community. These ways of interacting and communicating, combined with curricular materials that were based in a different culture, significantly reduced students' abilities to access what should have been learning opportunities.

MacDonald's administrative structure also excluded the community from participating in school-related decision-making processes. To begin with, the school was part of the larger school system and subject to its policies and hierarchies. Curriculum guidelines were a government matter, while local decisions were made by the authoritarian principal, by central office administrators, or by the local school board. On the school board, only the local priest represented the interests of the Innu. Sporadic efforts on the part of community members to influence school decisions generally fell on deaf ears. On one occasion, community members attempted to influence the hiring of a new vice principal. In response to a perceived threat to their authority, central office administrators came down in force to meet with members of the community. They told them in no uncertain terms that they as district administrators would be the ones making hiring decisions because they were paying the bills. These administrators conveniently overlooked the fact that they were getting additional money to support this school because of its Native clientele.

In the end, the effects of this exclusion were disastrous. Most students learned little. Those who did attempt to learn were sometimes made to feel bad about their less-than-successful efforts.[6] Many missed school for reasons other than the fall hunt. Many others simply dropped out. Of the cohort of eighteen that began first grade in 1970, only three made it to tenth grade.[7] Few came away from the school with skills that would provide them with opportunities for employment when they left. For others, the school experience, while less than successful in itself, turned them away from their own culture. At the time, the Innu were powerless to do anything about this state of affairs because they were excluded from decision-making processes. To be sure, change did come in the 1990s, but only after the community took drastic action. The government finally gave in to community pressure and agreed to give the community control of the school after parents took the extreme measure of taking their children out of school.[8]

The exclusive practices at Peter MacDonald School in the 1980s were perhaps a little more evident than they would be in most contemporary schools in the Western world. Most schools, however, are also exclusive, at least in some respects—for example, in how they exclude students both physically and socially through processes such as suspension and expulsion. Suspension and expulsion rates in the United States and the United Kingdom are alarmingly high.[9] In the United Kingdom, schools have formally expelled as many as 12,700 students in a single year.[10] Some groups are more vulnerable to exclusion than others. For example, in the United Kingdom, eight out of ten students who are expelled are males and one in four are in the care of local authority—that is, foster care. Also, in the United Kingdom, "Black and ethnic students" are six times more likely to be formally expelled than white students.[11] The same is true for U.S. schools, which suspended or expelled 15 percent, 20 percent, 35 percent, and 38 percent of their respective white, Hispanic, African American, and Indian/Alaskan Native student populations in 1999.[12] Students can also choose to remove themselves occasionally or permanently. Those who do this are generally youths who find themselves excluded from other aspects of school activities and learning processes.

More commonly, students are subtly excluded from learning processes. One way to understand this type of exclusion is in terms of "cultural capital."[13] Cultural capital can be thought of as a set of valued resources. These include, among others, the ability to talk, act, and think in particular ways. According to this explanation, schools reward students who can do these things. Those who possess this cultural capital will be able to take advantage of the best learning opportunities. Those who do not have these resources will find that they are unable to access learning in the same way. This capital, however, is not a neutral or universal commodity; not all students come to school with it. For example, Pierre Bourdieu, the researcher who coined the phrase, has shown that the cultural capital required by schools has an element of social class privilege.[14] It is, in fact, middle class. This does not bode well for those who are not from the middle class. Working-class students will have difficulty accessing the best learning opportunities because they bring resources that differ from those favored by schools. Their situation contrasts markedly with that of middle-class students, whose cultural capital generally meshes with that favored by schools; their ways of talking, acting, and thinking allow them access to the best learning experiences. But differences in cultural capital are not just class-based. As the Mac-Donald School example illustrates, they can also have an ethnic dimension, not to mention the additional dimensions of gender[15] and sexual orientation.[16] MacDonald students were routinely excluded from learning activities because they did not bring to school the kinds of language and interaction skills that were required in their classroom context. The central point here is that schools exclude some students from activities by requiring them to have attributes or resources associated with cultural capital that they do not possess.

Parents can also be excluded because they do not possess certain kinds of cultural capital. Take the case of the parent who had difficulty in school council meetings and who is further described in Chapter Three. This individual reported that he had difficulty participating on an equal basis with the professional educators on the council because he was not familiar with the language, means of interacting, and contextual issues that related to the school. Exclusion emerges in two ways here. First, this man does not have the background knowledge and linguistic skills to understand what the educators are talking about. Second, his own unique understandings and capabilities are devalued by those who possess what are regarded as more valued assets in this particular context. Hargreaves notes how emotionally traumatic these experiences can be, for marginalized parents and students are regarded not only as less than they are but also more derogatively as objects of disgust.[17]

Schools also exclude students by featuring knowledge in the curriculum that some students may have trouble identifying with. In the case of MacDonald School, this was obvious. But all schools do this in some form or another. Knowledge is never universal or neutral. It will always be presented from a particular perspective and address a unique area of experience. It is not uncommon for school curricula to ignore aspects of community, indigenous, and spiritual knowledge.[18] Given the increasing levels of diversity in today's schools, it is inevitable that some aspects of students' knowledge will be absent.

Schools regularly exclude many from their processes of influence. Like many bureaucratic institutions in the Western world, schools are organized hierarchically. Those at the apex of the hierarchy have power over those in lower positions. This power is accompanied by a right to make decisions for others. Within the framework provided by Canadian legislation,[19] most school principals routinely make choices for teachers, students, and community members. This does not mean that administrators never share power. Many, of course, do, and the next chapter documents some of these efforts. But this sharing is not always evident when it is not required by legislation, particularly in view of the responsibility that accompanies power. Administrators may be reluctant to share power with others who do not assume the same burden of responsibility that they do, especially if those others lack the same level of expertise and experience or the same values. But as we have seen in the example of MacDonald School, for a school community to be truly inclusive, it has to extend inclusion to its processes of influence; it will be difficult for all students to be included in the best learning opportunities if their interests are not taken into account or fairly represented in decision-making processes.

Small wonder then, that exclusion and inclusion inevitably have an impact on important aspects of schooling. Perhaps most telling is the effect on the emotional health of students. When asked in one study how they felt when excluded, students responded that they felt angry, resentful, hurt, frustrated, lonely, different, confused, isolated, inferior, worthless, invisible, substandard, unwanted, untrusted, unaccepted, closed, and ashamed. On the other hand, they said that when they were included they felt proud, secure, special, comfortable, recognized, confident, happy, excited, trusted, cared about, liked, accepted, appreciated, reinforced, loved, grateful, normal, open, positive, nurtured, important, responsible, and grown-up.[20]

Schools routinely exclude students by excluding them physically as well as through selective learning processes, curricula, and authority structures. This exclusion is not random; plainly, it happens to certain groups more than others. Two things occur in the process of exclusion. First, differences are identified and boundaries are erected. People make distinctions between groups and the characteristics associated with them. In the case of MacDonald School, the differences between European North American culture and Innu culture were obvious. In other settings, these differences are not always so apparent. Second, values are attached to these differences. Characteristics associated with middle-class, Anglo or

European, male, heterosexual cultures are generally valued more than others. At MacDonald School, most properties associated with European-based North American culture were prized more than those relating to Innu culture. Elements of Innu culture were believed not to be valuable enough to be included in the school's activities, and they were excluded. This process also occurs routinely in most other schools.

Needless to say, exclusion is not unique to schools; it also occurs as a matter of course in local and global communities. The circumstances that dictate people's fortunes originate, in many respects, outside of school. Thus, what happens in local and global communities affects what happens in schools.[21] One place that exclusion operates is in the organization of contemporary work and in how it continues to generate cycles of poverty.

Exclusion, Poverty, and Work

Exclusion and poverty are related. Poor people are routinely excluded from opportunities to participate in both school and community activities. They do not have the power or the ability to experience what others in better financial positions can. In school, less well-off students are unable to consistently gain the better learning opportunities, and they suffer accordingly. If there is any one finding that researchers in education have agreed on over the years, it is that educational experiences and achievement are related to economic position.[22] The children of parents who are financially secure do better in school than the children of those who are not financially secure. Furthermore, the latter are more likely to drop out of school before graduation and less likely to go on to postsecondary education than their middle-class counterparts.[23] Those who do pursue education beyond the secondary level generally attend vocational institutions or colleges and take two-year programs.[24]

Poverty and exclusion are also related to what people do. The nature of their work determines their economic position and the degree to which they are able to participate in the life of their community. This is not new. It has been happening for many centuries. From feudal to modern times, people's fortunes have been associated with the occupation they pursue. Even when the industrial revolution ushered in new forms of labor, poorer people stayed poorer and richer people remained better off. This occurred because poorer people were generally paid less than what their labor was worth. Employers made money from their employees' labor and, in doing so, helped to maintain a significant gap between rich and poor. However, economies of the West that were based on large-scale manufacturing enterprises did make some progress in reducing inequalities between rich and poor as the mid-twentieth century came and went. Salaries and conditions of the working class gradually improved over the years, and a middle class emerged and grew.[25] This progress, however, has now come to an abrupt halt.

In both the United States and the United Kingdom, the gap between the rich and poor has steadily increased since the 1970s, despite the fact that changing systems of production in North America and Europe may operate differently.[26] In the United States, most people in the bottom two-thirds of income distribution have seen their wages decline.[27] The income share of the lowest one-fifth of wage earners decreased from 4.4 percent in 1974 to 3.5 percent in 2001, while the income share of the top 5 percent increased from 15.9 percent to 22.4 percent. Moreover, the lowest one-fifth brought in 3.5 percent of the total income, while the highest one-fifth took in 50.1 percent.[28] From 2002 to 2003, poverty rates increased. The number of people below the official poverty threshold numbered 35.9 million in 2003, 1.3 million more than in 2002, for a 2003 poverty rate of 12.5 percent, while the number of families in poverty increased from 7.2 million (9.6 percent) in 2002 to 7.6 million (10.0 percent) in 2003.[29] The distribution of financial worth represents an even starker difference between the rich and the poor. In 1995, 1 percent of the U.S. population owned 47.2 percent of financial assets, and 20 percent owned 93.0 percent. On the other end of the spectrum, the bottom 40 percent owned less than nothing: −1.3 percent of this same pie.[30] Ironically, profits for U.S. businesses have never been higher.[31] The same is true for Canada and the United Kingdom. In Canada, the latest numbers indicate that the gap between the rich and the poor has increased dramatically over the past two decades. Those with income levels in the top 10 percent saw the midpoint of their worth jump by 35 percent during this time, while the proportion of families with no net worth rose from 10 percent in 1986 to 16 percent in 1999.[32] In the United Kingdom, income for the lowest 10 percent of the population has decreased 25 percent, while the income of the top 10 percent has increased by more than 60 percent.[33]

One reason for this reversal of fortune is the change in the nature of work. Shifts in production over the past fifty years have left more people than ever excluded because there is now less need for the working poor.[34] At one time, many bodies were needed to do the routine tasks that kept factories running. This is no longer the case, at least not to the same extent, since technology now accomplishes many of the tasks that human beings once did. As well, many companies have expanded internationally, so when labor costs get too high, they just move their operations to distant lands. Changing work patterns have also contributed to the decreased need for workers. The economy no longer revolves around large-scale manufacturing. Instead, it relies more on flexible production and service industries. This allows companies to hire people for limited periods of time, to pay them lower wages, and to give them fewer benefits. More and more people today are being forced to accept part-time, temporary, and low-paying work. Although they are not completely excluded from the economy, many have only a marginal position within it. Low wages, insecure employment, and dependence on benefits and supplements such as welfare and unemployment insurance also make it difficult for many people to participate socially and politically in their communities.

The most glaring form of contemporary exclusion is spatial; people are excluded by virtue of where they live. Within cities, the poor are increasingly separated from the rich. Anyone who lives in an urban area in North America can attest to these divisions. Chicago, for example, has displayed growing polarization over time. Stable middle-class neighborhoods have been transformed into transient working-class ones.[35] Those who are forced to live in the less desirable locations have less access to crucial goods and services. Most important to our discussion is the lack of access to high-quality schools. For many people, where they live determines the kind of schooling their children will receive, and that determines much of those children's future life course. Given the lack of resources and other difficulties that many urban schools face, students who live in these areas typically experience poorer-quality education than those in more affluent areas. Inner-city schools are particularly disadvantaged. Not only are they are plagued by an inability to attract talented educators, but they often do not have the resources to maintain their buildings. A report commissioned by the Newark School System, for example, found that "Physical conditions in most of the schools observed by the comprehensive compliance team reveal . . . neglect and dereliction of duty. Holes in floors and walls; dirty classrooms with blackboards so worn as to be unusable; filthy lavatories without toilet paper, soap or paper towels; inoperable water fountains; . . . and foul smelling effluent running from a school into the street, speak of disregard for the dignity, safety, basic comfort and sense of well-being of students and teachers."[36]

Work, poverty, and exclusion are intimately related to education. The increasing number of people who must take part-time, temporary, or poorly paid work find themselves excluded from participating in many things that their communities have to offer. This has at least two consequences for education. First, students from poorer families are excluded from many learning experiences at school. Jean Anyon's classic work from the early 1980s illustrates how different approaches to curriculum content can produce very different experiences.[37] The teachers she studied in two working-class elementary schools excluded their students from conceptual, varied, challenging, and wide-ranging material (material that their higher-class counterparts in other schools received) by focusing on basic skills, repetition, a limited range of topics, and practical knowledge. The view of knowledge in these schools is not knowledge as concepts, cognitions, information, or ideas about society, language, or history, connected to principles or understandings of some sort. Rather, what constitutes school knowledge in those schools is (1) fragmented facts, isolated from context and connections with each other, with wider bodies of meaning, or with activity or biography of the students; and (2) knowledge of "practical," rule-governed behaviors—procedures by which the students carry out tasks that are largely mechanical. Sustained conceptual or academic knowledge has only occasional, symbolic presence in such schools.[38]

Anyon's more recent work illustrates that nothing much has changed in the interim.[39] Other developments, however, have exacerbated these inequities in other ways. One of these is the trend toward marketization.[40] Simply put, the marketization of schools occurs when school systems favor practices that allow them to operate like markets. To do this, they make school boundaries permeable while expanding options for parents and their children. This means that parents or students are not obliged to attend a particular school; they can choose from a range of schools. Two spin-offs of marketization increase inequities. First, in order to make themselves attractive to potential "clients," schools engage in the practice of "skimming the cream." That is, they choose only those students whom they feel will boost their performance and, in turn, make them attractive to more potential clients. Not only do they select those who are likely to excel academically, but they also tend *not* to choose working-class and nonwhite students.[41] Second, marketization tactics also have consequences for other schools. The more successful ones tend to perpetuate their own success by attracting the best students. In doing so, however, they draw the better students from other schools in the area. Michael Baker and Martha Foote have illustrated this in their account of the city of "Bradford." They show how the attractive magnet school in the area drew the best students from another school, which steadily declined as the magnet school prospered.[42]

The neighborhoods in which many poorer families are forced to live have schools that do not offer what suburban schools are able to give their students. Chronic shortages of resources and less adequate facilities are common in schools that serve poorer communities.[43] But it is not just the poor who are excluded from school and community life. Men, women, and children who belong to ethnic groups that are not of European heritage are also regularly left behind.

Exclusion, Ethnicity, and Reactions to Diversity

Exclusion also occurs across ethnic lines. Those who are not of European or Anglo heritage in Western countries like the United States, the United Kingdom, Canada, and Australia are often excluded from community affairs and school learning experiences. Peter MacDonald School illustrates how this occurs in schools. In that case, the knowledge, language, and community experiences of the local people were not included in the curriculum, pedagogy, and leadership activities of the school; educators simply did not value them enough. This occurs routinely in many other schools, although it may not be as apparent, given the numbers and kinds of ethnicities involved. The result of this exclusion is that many students either drop out of school or fail to master the curriculum. This exclusion is not restricted to schools and is driven, at least in part, by racism. Racism is as much a problem as it ever was, surfacing in ever more subtle guises in an increasingly diverse world.

Exclusion has become more troubling as ethnic diversity continues to increase in Western countries. This diversity is not all the same. In some areas, immigration is swelling the number of different groups, while in other areas, it is not so much the number of different ethnicities but the size of just a couple of groups that is increasing. Canada, for the most part, represents an example of the former, while the United States, or at least parts of it, reflect the latter. Since the late 1960s, Canada has been receiving immigrants from all over the world. Before that time, most immigrants arrived from Europe—in particular, from the United Kingdom. Many of the new immigrants have settled in the larger cities, like Toronto, and the wide range of ethnicities is represented in local schools. Many urban and suburban schools in the Toronto area have upwards of sixty different ethnicities in their student body.[44] The United States has also been admitting people from places other than Europe over the past three decades. The more striking aspect of U.S. diversity, however, is not the number of different groups but the increasing numbers of blacks and Hispanics.[45] As of 2000, people of African American and Hispanic heritage each represented 16.6 percent of the total U.S. population.[46] In public schools, the number of students classified as "minority" increased from 29.3 percent in 1988 to 38.7 percent in 2000.[47] The West and South had the highest concentrations of minority students: 49 percent and 45 percent of the total student population, respectively.[48]

The fallout from ethnically based exclusion from schools is clear: more students who are not from the majority culture drop out and perform less well than their majority culture counterparts.[49] They are overrepresented in general and vocational tracks[50] and attend colleges and universities in proportionately fewer numbers than their Anglo brethren in the United States.[51] While there are exceptions to this pattern, these exceptions are not as universal as some may think.[52] Although minority student achievement has improved over the years, the gap between white students and others has leveled off recently and, in some cases, has begun to increase again. These trends are reflected in the achievement scores of Hispanic and black students in the United States. Both black-white and

Hispanic-white National Assessment of Educational Progress (NAEP) and Scholastic Achievement Test (SAT) score gaps narrowed by the early 1980s. By the late 1980s and early 1990s, however, these gaps had either stabilized or widened.[53] It appears, therefore, that many students have to work harder than others to attain the same levels of achievement.[54]

Exclusive practices show up in the classroom in many ways. Curricula, for example, routinely leave out relevant perspectives. Denise, a Canadian student of African heritage who eventually dropped out of the school system, comments on how the history classes she took made little mention of the contribution of black people: "The curriculum . . . was one-sided, especially when it came down to history. There was never a mention of any Black people that have contributed to society. . . . I mean, everything, it's the White man that did. History is just based on the European Canadians that came over. . . . There was no mention of the Africans that helped build a rail-way, that ran away from the South and came up to Nova Scotia and helped work and build Canada too . . . no mention of that.[55]

Behind the educational underachievement and general exclusion of minorities is a phenomenon that many majority culture members are uncomfortable acknowledging: racism. Racism is not just a set of overtly negative beliefs and actions that are directed toward particular groups. It can also be subtle, showing up in the actions of well-meaning individuals—for instance, teachers who patronize certain groups of students. Racism is also more than something individuals do or think. It is an integral part of general patterns, trends, and institutional practices and beliefs that transcend individuals. These patterns may find expression in laws, school regulations, behavior codes, and general or accepted habits of thinking, believing, and doing. The values that are integral to these beliefs and practices, however, routinely penalize and exclude certain groups and individuals from the experiences that others are able to enjoy.

One way in which these beliefs find concrete expression is in stereotypes. The stereotypes that are held at Suburbia Secondary School, a diverse secondary school in a rapidly growing suburban area of a large North American city, are typical.[56] Both students and teachers subscribe to the belief that Asian students are academically gifted. Trina is typical of many other teachers when she says that "the Chinese, the Japanese, they all sit together at the front. They're bright, very bright. Brilliant."[57] On the other hand, many feel that while students of African heritage are gifted physically, they are lacking in intellectual abilities. As a consequence, African male students sometimes feel pressure to join sports teams, while both black males and black females say that they have to work harder than other students to achieve comparable marks. Maria, for example, says, "You have to work twice as hard as every other kid in your class [to do well]. It shouldn't be that way."[58] Unfounded beliefs about groups of people, whether positive or negative, make it more difficult for people from those groups to be included in learning in meaningful ways.

Racist beliefs and practices continue to exclude many people from both community and school life. This exclusion was more obvious in the past; not so long ago, blacks in the United States were denied citizenship and education privileges.[59] This is no longer the case; African Americans now have the same rights and privileges as whites, at least in principle. In practice, however, blacks are still excluded from many privileges. For example, they do not have the same opportunities as others in the job market, even if they possess equal or superior skills.[60] Blacks are also treated differently by the justice system. A study in Toronto, for example, revealed that whites picked up on simple drug possession charges were released on the scene in exchange for a promise to appear in court at a later date 76.5 percent of the time, while blacks were released only 61.8 percent of the time. Of those taken to a police station, blacks were held for a court appearance 15.5 percent of the time, while only 7.3 percent of whites were kept.[61] Other evidence confirms this trend.[62]

Recent reactions to increasing levels of diversity also threaten to exclude people of non-Western heritage from community life. Some see diversity as a direct threat to their communities. They believe that efforts to recognize or include other cultures or ethnicities can only result in fragmentation and conflict. In the United States, Arthur Schlesinger believes that what he refers to as the contemporary "cult of ethnicity" will leave his country "a society fragmented into ethnic groups." In his view, acknowledgment of diversity "exaggerates differences, intensifies resentments and antagonisms, drives deeper the awful wedges between races and nationalities." Such a course risks "the disintegration of the national community, apartheid, Balkanization and tribalization."[63]

Others are even more definite about their wishes to exclude different others from their communities. Although their focus may be on preserving the sanctity of their community, their talk is clearly exclusionary. Adopting a fortress mentality, they emphasize patriotism, nationhood, and nationalism. Strategies for accomplishing such exclusion vary. In Europe, those who look to reinforce a distinct community identity may appeal nostalgically to the past. In Germany, for example, in an attempt to carve out a unique national identity, promoters of German culture refer longingly to *Heimat*— a mythical or idealized home or homeland. Reference to it is intended to get fellow Germans to identify with a common set of beliefs and a home that they share with these fellows. But this appeal is as much about exclusion as it is inclusion. According to Morely and Robbins's book *Spaces of Identity: Global Media, Electronic Landscapes and Cultural Boundaries*, this strategy is about

> conserving fundamentals of culture and identity. And, as such, it is about sustaining cultural boundaries and boundedness. To belong in this way is to protect exclusive and therefore excluding identities against those who are seen as aliens and foreigners. The "Other" is always and continuously a threat to the security and integrity of

those who share a common home. Xenophobia and fundamentalism are opposite sides of the same coin. For indeed *Heimat*-seeking is a form of fundamentalism. The apostles of purity are always moved by the fear that intermingling with a different culture will inevitably weaken and ruin their own.[64]

The exclusionary frame of mind in the United States is also reflected in the writing of Pat Buchanan. He maintains that "for the first time since Andrew Jackson drove the British out of Louisiana in 1815, a foreign enemy is inside the gates, and the American people are at risk in their own country."[65] For him, real Americans are not those of African, Hispanic, or Asian heritage but only those of Western—that is, European—heritage. Non-Europeans are the enemy, and they threaten not only his precious state but the whole of Western civilization. Buchanan believes that if something is not done to stem the "immigration tsunami rolling over America," it will become a Third World state. Whether or not we regard Buchanan's words as racist, his desire to exclude those who are not of European heritage from his American community is obvious.

The type of exclusion that Buchanan advocates has threatened to become more than just rhetoric in the wake of the terrorist attacks of September 11, 2001. The emotion of that moment has given way to responses designed to prevent this sort of tragedy from ever occurring again. Unfortunately, some of the measures target certain groups and threaten to exclude them from aspects of community life in the United States. Among other things, the new security measures extend the racial profiling that was already under way before the attacks.[66] Muslims and people from Arab countries have been targeted, attacked, and watched. As many as one thousand serious attacks were committed against people perceived to be Muslims or Arabs, and up to 11,000 immigrants were detained in the aftermath of the September 11 attacks.[67] Moreover, new legislation now permits increased surveillance of these and other groups and individuals that officials feel to be threats to U.S. national security. The USA Patriot Act of 2001 increases the power of law enforcement officials to conduct surveillance, order wiretaps without public disclosure, carry out secret searches, and detain immigrants indefinitely. The Patriot Act also authorizes the Central Intelligence Agency to spy on American citizens, conduct secret immigration trials, and monitor privileged attorney-client exchanges.[68]

The new security measures make it difficult for some groups to enter the United States in ways that Buchanan would likely approve of. They discourage many people with some connection to Arab countries and others who are political activists. Professor Javad Mostaghimi is one such person.[69] Born in Iran, he completed master's and doctoral degrees at the University of Minnesota before settling in Canada in 1982. A respected scholar, Canada research chair (a position designed for accomplished scholars), and vice dean, he was invited not long ago by the National Science Foundation to present a paper at a workshop in the United States. He declined when he learned what would be expected of him at the Canada-U.S. border. New U.S. legislation requires Canadian citizens born in Iran, Iraq, Libya, Sudan, or Syria to be fingerprinted, photographed, and questioned each time they enter the United States. After learning of these requirements, Mostaghimi said, "I declined to be treated like a criminal and cancelled my visit altogether. . . . I have decided not to travel to the U.S. again until such time as I am welcome."[70]

Exclusion, Gender, and Sexual Orientation

Exclusion also surfaces in gender and sexual orientation relationships. These types of exclusions, however, appear to be less of a concern than they once were; females and gay people are often seen as being included in more aspects of life than ever before. Women and girls are included in greater numbers in activities, occupations, and institutions once reserved primarily for their male counterparts. One of these areas is in the administration of schools. More women now occupy administrative positions in school districts than at any previous time.[71] One school district near where I live reflects this trend; it has more female than male administrators. The top administrative position is held by a woman, and so are two-thirds of the central office positions. Moreover, women hold principalships in half of the secondary schools and close to two-thirds of the elementary schools in the district. Pundits have pointed to other kinds of progress, like the recent academic achievements of girls,[72] in order to claim that there is no longer any need to be concerned with gender issues.[73] This sentiment has been displayed in government moves to stop such things as the collection of equity statistics.[74]

Perceived progress on the part of gay men and women has also brought about a kind of complacency. Once labeled as flawed human beings,[75] gay people are now openly celebrating their sexuality and being accepted in greater numbers than ever before. In many places, laws and regulations guarantee rights such as freedom from discrimination; an increasing number of forums allow gay people to freely express their sexuality—for example, gay pride parades are more common these days; and the public tolerates the presence of gay people in ways that it has never done before. In Canada and Massachusetts, despite opposition and subsequent backlash, court decisions have cleared the way for gay people to marry, and more than a few have taken advantage of this opportunity.[76] But despite this progress, there is still cause for concern. Women, girls, and gay people are still marginalized and excluded in ways that men and heterosexual people are not.

Women continue to be excluded from the best jobs. While they have made progress in the job market, overall, the positions that they hold pay less and have less power and status than those held by their male counterparts. Demonstrable gains in the status of women are misleading because they are skewed by a small number of women who have entered the professions. Most women do not have access to such positions and the benefits that accompany them.[77] As a result, women tend to be poorer than men. This is particularly the case for single mothers. In the United States, 52 percent of poor families were headed by women in 1989, compared with 23 percent in 1959.[78] In the Western world, households headed by female single parents are more likely than those headed by men or married women to be poor.[79] The cause of this poverty is not welfare dependency, as some contend, but the nature of the jobs available to and forced upon single mothers.[80] The flexible work patterns favored by contemporary employers, which feature part-time, temporary, or subcontracted work leave these women particularly vulnerable to exploitation. According to David Harvey, "Not only do the new labor market structures make it much easier to exploit the labor of women on a part-time basis, and so to substitute lower-paid female labour for that of more highly paid and less easily laid-off core male workers, but the revival of sub-contracting and domestic family labour systems permits a resurgence of patriarchal practices and homeworking."[81]

The same type of exclusion appears in jobs in the field of education. Women tend to gravitate toward increasingly flexible employment options, in part to alleviate the stress related to job intensification—that is, the expectation that they do more in less time.[82] In the past, women chose alternatives to full-time work as a way of accommodating their domestic demands. Because they had few flexible options, many women gave up their full-time contracts to spend time at home with their children. Now, more school districts offer women the option of working under a part-time contract. Districts hire lower-paid newer teachers, the majority of whom are women, on part-time contracts, as a cost-saving measure.[83] This in turn increases the number of part-time workers, emphasizing the disparity between core and casual workers.

Although women have made inroads into administration in education, they do not hold as many positions as some may believe. Women are especially underrepresented in senior administrative positions; they hold only a small percentage of these positions in

Canada and the United States.[84] After an increase in the early 1990s, the number of women in central office positions has now begun to decrease.[85] Nevertheless, the number of women in school site administration is increasing. Men, however, still hold the majority of positions, even in elementary schools; recent data from Canada show that 31 percent of principals and vice principals of elementary schools are women, even though 65 percent of the teachers in those schools are women.[86] At the secondary level, the numbers of women are even lower. Women hold only one in five secondary school principalships and three out of ten vice principalships in Canada.[87] In the United States, the story is much the same. Although the number of women administrators is increasing, it continues to lag behind the number of male administrators, despite the greater number of women educators. As of 2000, women held 44 percent of the administrative positions, although they held 70 percent of the teaching jobs.[88] It is interesting that more women are coming into administrative positions at a time when such jobs are becoming more intense, complex, and uncertain and, consequently, less attractive.[89]

Women and girls are often excluded in other ways besides being denied employment opportunities. One of the most forceful ways is through sexual harassment. Despite efforts to eradicate sexual harassment, women and girls in schools still experience it on a regular basis.[90] Even at the elementary level, girls often have to endure various misbehaviors associated with sexual harassment.[91] Women educators may also experience sexual harassment. Amanda Datnow describes a case in which a group of male teachers used crass sexist discourse to disrupt reforms that they opposed.[92] Seeking to undermine the authority and control of women who were leading the reform efforts, the "good old boys," as they were known in the school, characterized the women as less committed to their job, called the reforms "women's work," and made sexist jokes about the women in public contexts. Although the filing of sexual harassment suits put an end to the sexist jokes, the struggle continued. The men eventually brought a stop to the reforms by using their connections to get the support of outside people (men) with power.

Gay men and women, despite marginal progress in the past few years, continue to be excluded in ways that straight people are not. Seven-year-old Brian, the son of a friend of mine, was having a lot of trouble sleeping, the result of higher-than-usual levels of anxiety. After much prompting, Brian finally told his father what the trouble was. The previous year, when he was six, Brian had mimicked words from a popular song, words that he undoubtedly did not understand, in front of a couple of friends. One of his companions, Paul, had immediately picked up on the words and called Brian a fag. Paul had then gone to a teacher and had told her what Brian had said. The teacher had then admonished Brian—and not Paul—for saying what he had said. The next year, the issue had resurfaced, with Paul repeating what Brian had said, ridiculing him in the process. Now seven years old and with a better understanding of the meaning behind the ridicule, Brian became very upset, so much so that his sleep patterns were interrupted.

Here is a more shocking example. Jamie Nabozny knew by the age of thirteen that he was gay.[93] Many others were also aware of his sexual orientation, and from seventh through tenth grade, Nabozny was repeatedly attacked. He was spat and urinated on, punched, and subjected to a mock rape. In the tenth grade, he was beaten so badly that he needed surgery to stop the internal bleeding and repair extensive abdominal damage. During one period, the abuse became so bad that he attempted to take his life on two separate occasions. All this occurred with the knowledge of administrators and teachers, most of whom did little to stop the abuse. The attitude of the administrators was that he had brought it all on himself. Eventually, in his junior year, Nabozny dropped out after administrators told him he should go to school elsewhere.

Unfortunately, these incidents are not isolated. They happen all too regularly. In the most severe cases, people are killed because of their sexual orientation.[94] But even though most gay students do not experience such extremes at school, nearly half of them don't feel safe when they are there. One poll indicated that 70 percent of gay students surveyed said they had been taunted, sexually harassed, shoved, kicked, punched, and even beaten.[95] Another study reported that 97 percent of students had heard homophobic comments from their classmates, and 57 percent had heard similar comments from school staff.[96] This violence haunts gay young people not only on school grounds but also in their homes, where family members often abuse them because of their sexual orientation.[97] Such conditions can have devastating consequences for young people. The U.S. Department of Health and Human Services indicates that one in three lesbian and gay youths attempts suicide, and one in four has serious substance abuse problems.[98] At school, they display many of the problems that other high-risk groups do. They tend to have discipline problems, and they often find that the school curriculum is irrelevant to their personal needs, family-related problems, and issues with self-esteem and personal security.[99]

Gay educators also suffer from the effects of homophobia. As recently as the 1960s, Florida and California school officials conducted witch-hunts to weed out gay teachers.[100] In the 1980s, being suspected of being gay put one at risk of termination.[101] Not surprisingly, both teachers and administrators are reluctant to advertise their sexual orientation if it is not heterosexual. Melissa, a participant in Fraynd & Capper's study of sexual minority administrators, shares why she doesn't advertise her sexual orientation: "We have a pocket of very conservative people. I know who they are. . . . They would fire me even if they suspected, or if they had more to go on . . . they would run me out. . . . I wouldn't want to be taken out of education at this level because of that. . . . I don't have a guarantee right now that I wouldn't be."[102]

The administrators who conceal their sexual identity experience considerable stress from the risk of slipping up and being exposed. On the other hand, those who declare themselves feel that they have to perform at exceedingly high levels. Randy, another administrator in the same study, says, "The hardest part is that I have to be a flawless principal to be taken seriously. Now, if I were straight and advocating for [sexual minority students], it would be different. But, when I am criticized, I've got to take the power away from them of criticizing me professionally. So, it puts a lot of pressure on me to not make mistakes in my role as principal because I am gay."[103]

Multiple Exclusions

It would be misleading to think of exclusion as something restricted exclusively and permanently to any one of the aforementioned categories. Exclusion works in more complicated ways. The various kinds of exclusion regularly overlap with one another, and they may affect individuals and groups in different and fluid ways. This means that a person may be subject to more than one type of exclusion at the same time. Single mothers are one example. Single mothers are excluded on the basis of both gender and class; through double exclusion, they are left out of the opportunities and privileges that males and those with more financial resources generally enjoy. The consequences of exclusion increase even more in instances in which single mothers are not members of the majority ethnic group. The U.S. Census reveals that blacks and Hispanics suffer noticeably higher levels of poverty than whites. In 2002, 32.3 percent of blacks and 27.7 percent of Hispanics were below the poverty line, as opposed to 7.4 percent of whites.[104]

Individuals may experience both exclusion and privilege at the same time. For example, poor males may be excluded by their class position yet enjoy the advantages that come from being a male in certain contexts. The same is true of middle-class women; they are excluded because of their gender yet privileged because of their class. In a similar vein, young males of African heritage may suffer exclusion in schools because of race relationships yet experience advantages in some contexts because of their gender.[105] Exclusion tends to get even more complicated when it is considered on an international scale. Mexico and Mexican Americans tend to suffer disadvantages when dealing with U.S. institutions, while indigenous people living in Mexico are excluded in many ways.[106] Citizens of Japanese descent were interned in North America during World War II, and people in Japan currently exclude Koreans. The Western world persecutes people from the Middle East, while a number of Middle Eastern cultures exclude women from many privileges. The West does not have a monopoly on exclusion; it is pervasive, existing in all societies and settings. Individuals occupy a range of different identities and, as a result, may experience both inclusion and exclusion, depending on the circumstances that they find themselves in. Whatever the case, the challenge for leadership is to search out these multiple and complex forms of exclusion, expose them for what they are, and work to change them.

Exclusion and Contemporary Leadership Perspectives

People can be regularly and unfairly excluded from school and community life on the basis of their economic position, ethnic background, gender, sexual orientation, and so on. They can also be excluded by leadership practices in schools, either by being left out of leadership and influence processes themselves or by suffering under leadership practices that endorse or work toward values that do not favor inclusion.

I will now review three widely advocated and adopted approaches to leadership—managerial/technical, humanistic, and transformational perspectives—and show how they are, at least in some respects, exclusive. Although these perspectives do not always correspond with what people actually do and although individual leaders rarely display characteristics that are associated with just one perspective, it is nevertheless useful to look at these perspectives separately, in their ideal form, for all of them are influential in leadership practice.

These and other leadership perspectives can be exclusive by virtue of the type of relationships they prescribe, the ends to which leadership practices are geared, and the manner in which leadership practices are treated. Perspectives that advocate relationships that assume some people's right to make decisions for others can be exclusive. Assuming that holding a position in an organization or having apparent expertise gives some people rights over others can exclude some from exerting influence on what happens in a given setting. Seeing leadership as an individual as opposed to a group process necessarily excludes some people from the process. Leadership processes can also exclude people if they are not organized to promote inclusion in general. Perspectives that leave the ends of leadership open or focus on promoting organizational ends such as efficiency will not be legitimately inclusive if they do not also work toward inclusion. Leadership perspectives need to advocate for particular ends, such as inclusion.

The same critiques apply to various forms of inquiry. Research that merely describes what leaders do, as in some of the humanistic approaches, stand less chance of generating insights that will help promote inclusion than approaches that are organized to achieve this end, because researchers who are committed to inclusion will be more sensitive to issues that both support and obstruct it than those researchers who are not focused in that way.

Managerial/Technical Leadership

My first exposure to the academic world of administration was enlightening, or so I thought at the time. Like many other graduate students in educational administration in the early 1980s, I was introduced to the wonders of science. Administration, I was taught, should be seen as a science. This science was believed to be capable of bringing order and certainty to the rough-and-tumble world of educational administration. It could do so, its advocates informed us, by telling leaders how to make decisions for the people who worked in organizations.[107] Decision making was to be left not to chance, individual whim, or personal preference but to a science that would prescribe preferred courses of action. If only administrators would approach leadership as a set of scientific techniques, they could avoid making the mistakes that would inevitably result when they exercised their own less-than-perfect judgment.

As comforting as this managerial/technical vision seemed at the time, it had many flaws.[108] Even the more contemporary versions, such as the new managerialism referred to in Chapter One, are problematic. The new managerialism has evolved partly as a response to declining revenues for public schools, the perceived problem of resistance on the part of educators and students to current practices and policies that they believe are not in the interests of students, and a desire by policymakers to seek public approval.[109] It is also a response to the unfounded perception that not all is well with schools and that educators are largely to blame for these problems. The new managerialism solution to these and other problems rests with market forces and technical management. Proponents of this view believe that unleashing market forces, often in the form of consumer choice, will free managers at the local level to do what they do best. They feel that these moves will allow administrators to focus on the important goals of effectiveness, efficiency, performance, and productivity. But because advocates of this position believe that local administrators are partly responsible for the mess that schools are in, they are unwilling to trust these administrators and their equally undependable teachers to act autonomously. Instead, proponents of the new managerialism see the need for policies that limit administrators' actions. To the proponents of the new managerialism, administration is a technical operation designed to execute policies that have been formulated elsewhere. New managers do not design, deliberate on, or question goals or policies; they merely see that they are put into practice. For example, they will be responsible for seeing that such initiatives as standardized testing and common curricula are put in place in their schools.

The managerial perspective on leadership excludes people in the way it envisions authority and the ends toward which it is geared. Authority is distributed exclusively by position. Advocates of managerial leadership believe that the best way to run organizations is to vest people in administrative positions with the authority to make decisions for others. People are distinguished by position, and their potential to influence what happens in organizations is related to their position. So an administrator or leader is much more involved in decisions and policymaking than those below him or her in the hierarchy. Those not in administrative positions or in the lower echelons of the hierarchy are all but excluded from efforts to influence the organization. In such scenarios, teachers, students, and parents and their views and perspectives are excluded from the influence processes at the school.

Managerial/technical approaches to leadership are also exclusive in the values they promote. They speak little to organizational goals other than to advocate that these goals, whatever they are, be pursued in the most productive and efficient ways possible. A managerial perspective is not concerned with underlying organizational values or goals; rather, its main function is to help administrators achieve already established ends. As absurd as it may seem, a school might actively or unwittingly pursue a program of exclusion, and managerial/technical approaches would have little to say about it. To be truly inclusive, leadership arrangements must explicitly work toward inclusion. Failing to do this, as leaders do in many managerial/technical scenarios, seriously jeopardizes inclusive goals and perpetuates injustice as a result.

Humanistic Leadership

It was not until later in my academic career that I was exposed to humanistic approaches to leadership in educational administration.[110] Regarded as less legitimate, they represented serious threats to the established scientific approaches and were therefore ignored by many. Only when I started my doctorate did I engage fully with the humanist position, learning about it firsthand from one of its pioneers in educational administration—Thom Greenfield. At the time, I thought it represented an exciting alternative to the sterile approach of scientific management.

Humanistic approaches represented a reaction to impersonal technical approaches. Whereas scientific approaches emphasized techniques, humanistic perspectives stressed the centrality of human beings. Advocates maintained that leaders were not moral ciphers or mere technicians but real people and that who they were affected how they approached their jobs. The values to which they subscribed, the meanings they attributed to situations, and the cultural milieu in which they worked influenced the decisions they reached. In this world of administration, humanity, not science, held sway. Not surprisingly, those who adopted this perspective concentrated their efforts on understanding the individuals who occupied the role of administrator and the circumstances in which they worked. Many scholars of humanistic leadership also emphasized description over prescription, at least in principle.

While humanistic approaches represented an advance over the managerial perspective, they were also exclusive. Advocates generally equated leadership with the position of leader. They presumed that administrators were different from others in organizations and that administrators had the power to influence people in ways others did not. Proponents of the humanistic view also acknowledged that the values of individual administrators could have an important impact on what they did and on the culture of their respective organizations. There is little in this perspective, however, that either acknowledged or advocated for the particular values and practices of inclusive leadership.

Perhaps the biggest obstacle to inclusion is the tendency of most—but not all—advocates of humanistic leadership to describe rather than prescribe. Many of these researchers are content merely to observe, conduct empirical studies, and theorize about leadership.

Granted, some do recommend particular strategies, but in the end, they fall short of identifying exclusion in ways that reveal its depth or advocating for inclusion in a manner that would counteract pervasive exclusive practices such as racism.[111] While the humanist perspective has been valuable in presenting a more realistic picture of what administrators really do, it has done little to advance the cause of inclusion.

Transformational Leadership

Transformational approaches to leadership are a more recent phenomenon in education. Advocacy for transformational leadership as the kind of leadership to which all should aspire has given it a high profile and widespread currency. Yet I will show that it can also be exclusive.

Transformational leadership borrows from both managerial/technical and humanistic approaches. It combines the prescriptive element of the former with the human side of the latter. In doing so, it draws on a long tradition in leadership inquiry. Although it is not to be equated with charismatic leadership, transformational leadership does emphasize the talents of particular individuals.[112] Transformational leaders are expected to use their considerable talents to raise the "level of human conduct and ethical aspiration of both leader and led,"[113] thus transforming both. Ideally, transformational leaders provide the following:

- Inspirational, charismatic leadership that increases follower motivation

- Individual consideration of followers that caters to their individual needs

- Intellectual stimulation that influences followers' thinking and imagination

- Influence, in ways that prompt followers to identify with their leader's vision

Leaders who are able to accomplish these feats are believed to be able to enhance the resources of both leader and led by raising their level of commitment to mutual purposes and by further developing their capacities for achieving these purposes.[114]

Despite benefits such as its inspirational character and the useful strategies it sets out for leaders, transformational leadership can still be exclusive.[115] Like managerial and humanistic approaches, it has little to say about the organizational goals for which leaders should be working. Transformational leaders could, at least in principle, be pursuing exclusive ends.

Transformational leadership also assumes that leaders can be distinguished from the led by virtue of the special attributes they bring. To be fair, proponents see transformational leaders as working with others and including them in decision-making and policymaking activities. Nevertheless, it is difficult to shake the impression that transformational leadership is in an important way a stand-alone enterprise because of the way in which the actions of a single gifted individual are so prominently featured.[116] This person is believed to be capable of single-handedly raising not only his or her own efforts but also the performances of all whom he or she is leading. Transformational leadership emphasizes the importance of talented individuals and thus implicitly excludes supposedly less talented others, even though the latter may at some point be involved in decisions. In doing so, it makes it more difficult to imagine or recognize leadership as a truly collective endeavor.[117] This is unfortunate because collective leadership practices can be very effective.[118] Research in schools has shown that collective enterprises have a much greater impact than the efforts of single individuals, regardless of how much positional power they have.[119] Collective leadership ideas and practices are also ideal for contexts of inclusion. They make it possible for a range of school community members to be involved meaningfully in decisions about fundamental schooling matters.

Conclusion

This chapter has explored the problem of exclusion. Exclusion occurs inside and outside of schools. In schools, students can be excluded physically. But even when they are physically present, they can still be excluded. This happens when they cannot identify with favored ways of interacting or with the school's favored forms of knowledge. Not random at all, exclusion follows distinct patterns. Members of school communities can be excluded by virtue of how they enter into relationships that center on gender, ethnicity, class, and sexual orientation. Of course, exclusion is not restricted to schools; it extends beyond them into local and global communities, and what happens in the world beyond schools has an impact on what happens in schools. Women, poor people, those who are not of European heritage, and gay men and lesbians find themselves excluded from opportunities and privileges that their counterparts regularly enjoy both in their communities and in schools.

Students and other members of school communities can also be excluded through leadership processes. Some leadership strategies are more exclusive than others. Although they are quite different, managerial/technical, humanistic, and transformational leadership approaches are exclusive. To varying degrees, they all see leadership as an individual and hierarchical enterprise. Leaders are distinguished from followers by virtue of the position they occupy or the skills they bring to their position, and they are expected to make decisions for others. Such approaches make it difficult to envision leadership as a collective and inclusive performance. These approaches also remain evasively neutral about the value of inclusion as a preferred goal of leadership.

Despite and in light of these obstacles to inclusion, researchers have studied and written about various forms of inclusive leadership in schools, and we have much to learn from them. The next chapter explores this literature.

3

The Evidence of Inclusive Leadership

We already know a great deal about inclusive leadership from practitioners and academics. Over the years, educators have tried out various kinds of inclusive leadership practices in their organizations, and researchers have studied these efforts and written and speculated about them, so there is no shortage of information. The challenge is sifting through the reams of material in ways that will help us to understand and promote inclusive leadership.

Most of the relevant literature in this chapter does not adopt the heading *inclusive leadership*, employing other names such as *teacher leadership, shared governance, participative leadership, student leadership, site-based management,*[1] *community involvement*, and *emancipatory* or *critical leadership*. The only group of studies that uses the phrase *inclusive leadership* uses the term *inclusive* to refer to the education of differently abled students. The articles and studies that I review below do not always fit easily into one category. Some belong in two and sometimes more categories. For the sake of clarity and convenience, the characteristics I attribute to the various leadership types are ideal. I use the various studies to clarify what I mean by these ideal types. While each standpoint represents only a partial and decidedly limited view of inclusve leadership, taken together, they provide considerable insight into it.

Remember that inclusive leadership emphasizes the process and product of leadership, in that

- All members of the community should be involved in influence processes.

- Leadership processes should promote inclusive practices generally.

Emancipatory Leadership

Proponents of emancipatory leadership advocate for a more comprehensive view of inclusion than other theorists. Not only do emancipatory champions (as critical theorists) want educational leadership processes to be inclusive, but they are also committed to working for more global forms of inclusion. They view leadership as only one element of a much wider concern with inclusion. Critical theorists rightly believe that this concern is warranted because our institutions and communities are deeply unfair; some people consistently enjoy advantages at the expense of others. The task for leadership is to get people to recognize these injustices and work together to change them; only then can people become truly emancipated. To do this, emancipatory proponents appeal to theory to help people understand and critique the status quo and assist them in eventually changing oppressive structures. This has proven to be a difficult task, however. There are few schools that actually practice this form of emancipatory leadership. Consequently, most of the studies in this area are theoretical and prescriptive and are not grounded in empirical evidence.

The theory that many critical theorists employ is a form of self-estrangement theory.[2] Dating back centuries, it portrays humans as fallen creatures. Critical theorists maintain that humans cannot recognize that the forms of life they have created—like capitalism, for example—are unfair. All is not lost, however. This theory goes on to say that if men and women can rid themselves of their blinders, they can take action that will enable them to penetrate the mystifying ideologies that currently bind them,[3] providing them with the individual and collective autonomy they need to control their own lives.

The humanist version of self-estrangement theory has taken many forms over the years. The earlier ones concentrated on the economy. Critical theorists maintained that the dominant economic system—capitalism—was unfair because a few individuals profited from the work of many. These few got the most out of life, while the vast majority had to make do with considerably less. Critical theorists believed that for this injustice to come to an end, people had to first recognize how unfair this was, then take action to change the system.[4] Later versions of this theory branched out to include the injustices associated with race, gender, and sexual orientation. What all these theorists had in common was a concern for the less fortunate. They all agreed that less fortunate individuals were not to be blamed for their situation. Rather, wider social structures such as capitalism, sexism, racism, and homophobia put these people at a disadvantage. Critical theorists recognized that people needed to be made aware of these processes so they could take action to change them.

These ideas were subsequently adapted and applied to education and, eventually, to leadership. Over the years, scholars have used them to illuminate the ways in which class, race, and gender hierarchies work in schools and to document the different effects of these hierarchies on students, teachers, parents, and governance processes. Emancipatory leadership advocates call for collective over individualistic forms of leadership, stress leadership's educative side, and emphasize the importance of dialogue. Some also acknowledge the difficulty of putting their ideas into practice.[5]

Critical theories of leadership are, for the most part, consistent with the ideals of inclusion. To begin with, they reject individual and hierarchical views of leadership. Critical theorists distrust the hierarchies that accompany bureaucratic forms of organization. They correctly point out that these kinds of arrangements both reflect and reinforce wider social hierarchies and injustices.[6] Some contend that these organizational hierarchies themselves display class and gender overtones.[7] Feminists have been the most articulate about this, arguing that this hierarchical division of labor is masculine in nature and criticizing the ideals of power and control that are part of this corporate management view.[8] Critical theorists also take issue with the heroic view of leadership. They point out that individual men and women who occupy positions of responsibility are seldom capable on their own of creating fundamental changes and producing new and better values. Few administrators are charismatic, but most can be competent. As a consequence, critical theorists call not for heroes but for modest men and women to step forward.[9]

In an inclusive spirit, critical theorists favor collaborative, reciprocal, and horizontal relationships over the more traditional management hierarchies. For them, leadership does not reside in a position or a person but in equitable, caring, and fluid relationships among various individuals.[10] In their view, everyone should have a voice and the opportunity to contribute in their own ways to what happens in schools. For this to occur, school communities need to nurture dialogue.[11] They need to work toward providing conditions that allow everyone to communicate with one another. Among other things, this requires that communities foster communicative virtues like tolerance, patience, an openness to giving and receiving criticism, and a willingness to admit mistakes, listen thoughtfully and attentively, reexamine one's own presuppositions and compare them with others', and reinterpret one's own concerns in a style that makes them comprehensible to others.[12] Dialogue is also crucial to the educative part of emancipatory leadership.[13]

Emancipatory leadership emphasizes the educative side of leadership. It is perhaps this aspect more than any other that sets emancipatory leadership apart from other leadership perspectives. Critical theorists contend that the work of leadership is more educational than managerial; it is not about charisma or acting decisively but about helping members of school communities to learn about the world and to search out alternatives to the status quo.[14] The educative part of emancipatory leadership is first and foremost concerned with critiquing existing patterns of privilege. This is necessary, according to critical theorists, because most people do not notice that many of the things that they and others do are harmful. They take them for granted.[15] The task for leadership, then, is to raise the consciousness of people so that they can recognize widespread and harmful exclusive practices like racism and sexism and do something about them. This requires that school communities perpetually raise questions about what they do and about the wider context within which learning and schooling occurs. Schools need to audit themselves, but these audits are not the kind that accountants do.[16] According to John Smyth, "Schools need to be involved in questioning what it is they are doing, not from an accountant's point of view, but from the perspective of how their agenda fits with a broader view of what constitutes a just society. If there is any auditing of schools deemed necessary, then it needs to be educational, moral and democratic forms of auditing."[17]

There are a number of reasons that it is difficult to find examples of emancipatory leadership practices in schools. Perhaps the most obvious is that educators work in culturally conservative institutions that value homogeneity, resist change, and look unfavorably on challenges.[18] Moreover, many of the people who can do the most to introduce this kind of leadership—most of them administrators—are themselves conservative, socialized into a system that rewards supporters.[19] An administrator's job is generally one that puts out fires rather than starts them. Regrettably, those who actually do adopt adversarial stances to force through progressive reforms may find themselves looking for work; many of the best adversarial leaders have been fired.[20] Challenging the system can be risky. So the answer is to set up leadership dynamics that are based not on the personality of a single individual but on processes that involve everyone.[21] This way such organizations can survive the loss of any single individual and be true to inclusive principles.

Instances of emancipatory leadership do exist, however. Few in number, they display some—but generally not all—of the elements expected of this type of leadership. Two examples display strengths in an area that is the least practiced—critique. Mr. G.'s School and Richmond Road School devoted their efforts to promoting critique within their respective school communities.

Mr. G.'s School

Mr. G.'s School serves a diverse elementary population in a rural area of a large urban school district.[22] Forty-five percent of the 72 percent Caucasian, 25 percent African American, and 3 percent Hispanic population qualify for reduced-price lunches. The school is Mr. G's second appointment as a principal. Now in his fourth year at the school, all of his educational experience has been at the elementary level. His school has spared no effort to enable the critique of individual and school practices. In doing so, the school has sought to support, facilitate, and provide possibilities for the people in the school community, which is one of the strategies used to create a supportive environment. The school pursues this strategy by providing autonomy with responsibility, shifting problem solving to teachers, and communicating its trust in them. In one instance, Mr. G. took advantage of an opportunity to shift problem-solving responsibility to teachers and then to students. Faced with a continuing problem with lunchroom noise and behavior, he brought it up at a staff meeting. After discussing the issue for some time, the staff came to the conclusion that it was not their problem but the students' problem. The teachers decided to present the problem to students through closed-circuit television and charge each classroom with coming up with a plan to correct their behavior. Students devised and implemented plans, and the lunchroom behavior improved.

In another instance, Mr. G. directly encouraged students to critique their own behavior and the problems associated with it. When the school first opened, students came from two schools; one was predominantly white, the other black. As time passed, racial tensions appeared to be escalating. In an effort to do something about the problem, Mr. G. called all the students to a meeting, and in the words of one teacher, they "talked and talked and worked out situations and had them critique situations: 'How would you solve that problem? Would that problem have occurred if that person wasn't black?' That really made them think about 'Why are you treating me this way?' "[23]

Mr. G.'s School also facilitated critical examination of teaching practice by requiring that teachers justify their practice—that they understand what they were doing and why. Mr. G. provided alternative frameworks for thinking about teaching and learning through staff development, making sure that all the teachers had the opportunity to attend workshops. He also had a habit of sharing professional articles with teachers, either placing them in mailboxes or circulating them at meetings. One teacher observed, "He conveys those things [i.e., what is important to him] through the materials he provides for us. . . . This morning I came in and in my mailbox was a box of file folders that said 'Happy Valentine's Day.' . . . He's constantly giving us articles to read. I mean, not 'Read this, there will be a test later.' but . . . 'You might find this interesting' or . . . 'If you're going to try a literature-based program, you might want to read this article.' "[24]

Mr. G. also made it possible for people to pursue alternatives to current practice by providing teachers with resources, encouraging grant writing, and soliciting donations of funds and materials. One of the teachers speaks of the positive spin-offs from the grant-writing process: "What's nice about grant writing is, we don't always expect to get the grant, but what it does is force you to sit down together to talk about programs that you might want to do if you could dream. . . . You organize your thoughts and then, whether you get the money or not, you find the money somewhere. I mean if you want to do it badly enough, you'll find the money somewhere. We always seem to."[25]

Although Mr. G.'s School did many positive things to help the school community critique its practice, it did not focus attention on unequal power relations other than principal-teacher relationships. Richmond Road School, on the other hand, did emphasize the power differences.

Richmond Road School

Richmond Road School in New Zealand acknowledged in no uncertain terms the role of power in the education of the multiethnic students in the school.[26] This was initiated in large part by the head teacher of the school, Jim Laughton. Of Maori heritage, he had come to understand firsthand the effects of power on marginalized people, and he sought to find ways to provide those without power access to it. One of the ways he did this was raising the consciousness of his teachers. In their weekly staff meetings, he would facilitate but not dominate critical discussions of academic articles. One local education official comments on the staff meetings:

> One of the things that I saw there that I never saw anywhere else, was the—here was a school with a built-in staff development programme . . . so that the staff meetings there, for instance—staff meeting seems such a pathetic name for what they did there—was such that there was this enforced sharing of knowledge. . . . I never saw that anywhere else at all. . . . I saw schools that had professional components in their staff meetings, but I didn't see one where it was built in . . . absolutely built in and implicit into the structure, totally into the structure of the school.[27]

Inevitably the conversations in staff meetings would touch on theory and issues of power. According to one of the teachers, these discussions engaged critical readings on power: "One was C. Wright Mills in *The Sociological Imagination* [1959]—'To those with power and are aware of it impute responsibility. To those with power but who are unaware of it, educate them and impute responsibility.

To those without power, inform them about what the others are up to!' So for him a lot of what we did was really about access to power . . . so that when you ask how children did that was actually one of his overriding concerns."[28]

These conversations had an impact on teachers, helping them to understand the more subtle aspects of power and to talk about them in lucid ways with their colleagues. One staff member said that

> Richmond Road School . . . is one of the few places I know of—maybe the only place I know of in terms of schools—that can hold a lucid debate about the way in which power works in the infant classroom. Again [to] most people power is something that exists "outside." . . . [Teachers at Richmond Road] can actually talk about it in terms of what teachers do with kids *inside* classrooms and they can talk about it . . . by taking a theoretical stance on it to begin with. "What . . . do we mean by power?" and then, "how does it work in this place? Is it quantifiable, and who's got it if it is? How do they use it?" The people in that school could talk like that and could deal with all those subjects.[29]

Richmond Road's critical approach to leadership generated many impressive outputs. The ideas about power eventually found their way into the workings of the school—for example, multiage groupings and curriculum modules that teachers would tailor for their unique student body. This critical approach to leadership also succeeded in raising the school community's consciousness about issues of equity and inclusion, which resulted in changes to its structure and programs that were designed to reverse the power differences that had initially existed. The school was able to do this, in large part, because of the charisma and drive of Jim Laughton. He was an enthusiastic and, at times, forceful champion of critical approaches to education. In fact, his personality was central to the

Richmond Road school community. One former teacher remembers that

> "Jim's personality was a major thing. . . . You cannot talk about Richmond Road without talking about Jim Laughton. You ask me what I carry with me; I carry the bold, bearded bugger sitting on my shoulder talking about bilingual education, because I remember you'd get into the office and then wouldn't get out for two hours because you'd end up with a discussion."[30]

But it was Laughton's prominent place in the school community that led to the demise of the school's novel approaches. Although he attempted to put structures in place that would succeed him, his charismatic and sometimes forceful approach to leadership made this institutionalization difficult. In hindsight, it is clear that his untimely death signaled the beginning of the end for these emancipatory practices because the school relied so heavily on him. The school that had shown so much promise as a model for multi-ethnic schools reverted back to traditional practices shortly after Laughton's successor, a former assistant head at Richmond Road, left to take up another position. Without those critical processes in place, it could not survive in an environment that was not supportive of many of its practices.[31]

Summary

The emancipatory leadership literature contributes many things to our knowledge of inclusive leadership—especially its balanced account of inclusive leadership, which attends to the process and the ultimate ends of leadership. In this view, leadership processes are just one part of a greater concern with inclusion. Leadership processes are organized not only to reflect inclusion within school governance structures but also to pursue it in communities and the world generally. Toward this end, leadership processes educate members of the school community to recognize forms of exclusion that are often hidden and to make changes that promote inclusion. The slim amount of evidence available and the more theoretical and prescriptive accounts point to ways in which school communities might do this. Dialogue is crucial. So too is the idea that leadership is best thought of not in terms of heroic individuals but as collective and equitable processes.

Emancipatory leadership approaches also display weaknesses. There is a significant gulf between theory and practice. Critical theorists rely heavily on theory and prescription, and this preoccupation sometimes blinds proponents to other insights and realities. At the same time, dependence on theory is also a result of there being so few examples of emancipatory leadership practices in schools. If inclusive leadership is to become a reasonable alternative, school communities need to take steps to embrace what can potentially be a misunderstood and threatening set of arrangements. Not everyone is likely to acknowledge criticism of current practice and embrace changes that may threaten them. For example, principals are generally reluctant to admit to the presence of racism in their school, and this affects the ways in which they respond to suggestions for change.[32] To increase the chances of positive change, leadership practices also need to be organized to advocate for inclusion, something that few address seriously.

Other areas of literature address a number of these shortcomings. First, they provide more detail on the unique circumstances associated with the inclusion of different groups of people in leadership processes. The literature on teacher and student leadership and parental involvement gives us insight into the circumstances surrounding the inclusion of these particular groups. Second, the more plentiful empirical studies in these areas supply evidence about leadership processes themselves, including what it means to include people in leadership processes, the reasons for and benefits of inclusion, the difficulties associated with inclusion, and the actions that help inclusive practice. Finally, this body of literature on leadership provides more detail on achieving the ultimate ends of leadership. In particular, the literature on leadership and inclusion of differently abled students presents a number of strategies for promoting inclusion.

Teacher Leadership

The literature on teacher leadership provides by far the largest body of work that touches on inclusion. It includes research on teacher leadership, shared governance, and participatory leadership. By definition, all of this work concentrates primarily on teachers. It also focuses almost exclusively on the process rather than the ends of leadership, exploring how teachers do or do not become involved in influence processes. In general, it does not attend to more global matters of inclusion and social justice.[33]

Most studies in this area examine experiments of teacher leadership in schools, of which there have been many in recent times. While teacher leadership has a long history, it has become a more common practice following the so-called second wave of reform, which, in contrast to previous calls for reform, advocated for fundamental changes in the governance structure of schools to enhance teachers' professionalism, autonomy, and empowerment.[34] Prompted in part by the recommendations of these reformers, many schools have initiated changes in their governance structures. By the late 1980s, just about every state in the United States had adopted or was studying some form of teacher leadership.[35] My task here is to examine those parts of the teacher leadership literature that help readers understand and promote inclusive leadership, especially the nature of teacher leadership, the problems associated with it, and the strategies employed to introduce, implement, and sustain it.[36]

What Is Teacher Leadership?

Despite all the research and differing views about what teacher leadership is or should be,[37] most research in this area agrees that the purpose of teacher leadership is to provide teachers with power in settings where traditionally they have not had it. The aim of this redistribution of power is to allow teachers to make decisions in a variety of areas that are relevant to their work[38] by participating in decision-making processes, having authority over professional issues at the classroom and school levels, and obtaining opportunities to acquire knowledge that warrants this authority.[39]

Teacher leadership can be formal or informal.[40] Informal leadership can occur outside of officially designated roles and responsibilities. It may include sharing expertise, volunteering for new projects, bringing new ideas to a school, helping colleagues carry out classroom duties, assisting in improvement of classroom practice, accepting responsibility for professional growth, promoting a school's mission, or working for improvement of a school and its system.[41] Teacher leadership may also involve other pursuits like conducting research in one's own classroom and school.[42]

Formal leadership generally involves teachers working in officially designated capacities. These positions may include acting as a department or division head, union representative, member of a school governance body, or representative of the school and district, among many others.[43] Perhaps the most attention in this area, however, has been given to initiatives that involve lead or master teachers, career ladders, and mentorship programs. Lead teacher positions are designed to allow particularly able teachers to develop curricular and instructional programs, organize staff development, and perform various administrative duties.[44] Career ladder programs emphasize job enlargement and new evaluation systems that provide opportunities for teachers to develop and implement projects that enhance student learning, improve a total school program, design curricula, and share expertise with teaching colleagues.[45] Teacher mentoring programs provide opportunities for experienced teachers to share their expertise with less experienced colleagues.

The nature of teachers' involvement in activities and decision making varies. The extent to which they may participate tends to be related to the nature of the issue, the degree to which their interests are affected, and their willingness to take risks that are associated with assuming responsibility.[46] Teacher involvement may be passive and hidden or overt and active.[47] Those who participate, however, do not always have influence. Teachers who sit on committees, for example, may not be able to influence in any meaningful way the decisions that are eventually made. These kinds of situations may prompt teachers to avoid or oppose opportunities for participation.[48]

One way of categorizing levels of involvement is in terms of a continuum that goes from autocratic (the principal makes decisions on his or her own) to information-sharing (the principal obtains information from teachers and makes decisions on his or her own) to consultative (the principal shares the problem and makes a decision that may or may not reflect teachers' views) to democratic (the principal shares the problem, analyzes it, and comes to a decision with teachers).[49] On the other end of the continuum, teachers make decisions on their own, after sharing information or after consultation.

There are many potential areas for teacher participation.[50] One typology, for example, specifies that teachers can become involved in decisions relating to curriculum and instruction, personnel, goal setting, student conduct, scheduling, extraschool relationships, and facilities.[51] Research indicates, however, that teachers are not always keen to participate in decisions that do not directly concern them. They prefer not to take part in more administrative types of decisions.[52] On the other hand, others maintain that teachers need to become involved in areas that are central to a school's health, such as choosing instructional materials, shaping curriculum, setting standards for student behavior, deciding whether students will be tracked in special classes, designing staff development, setting promotion and retention policies, deciding school budgets, evaluating teacher performance, and selecting new teachers and administrators.[53]

Why Teacher Leadership?

Many who write in the area of teacher leadership make cases for why it is a good thing. Fewer refer to its mixed blessings, and virtually no one recommends that teacher leadership be avoided. The cases that writers make can be classified as either practical or moral. The moral argument states that teacher leadership should be adopted because it is good for schools or because everyone should have the right to participate in influence processes, especially in decisions that affect their lives,[54] particularly in democratic countries.[55] Others maintain that teaching is a moral activity, and for moral agents to be responsible for their acts, they must be free to act according to their best judgment and not have others make decisions for them.[56]

Writers also encourage schools to embrace teacher leadership for practical reasons. Their argument is that teacher leadership will improve the ways that schools work; however, these claims are not consistently supported by the evidence. Studies that explore the relationship between teacher leadership and organizational effectiveness and student achievement are inconclusive.[57] The same holds for the effects on relationships within the school community.[58] The most consistent results concern the positive effects of teacher leadership on teachers' demeanor and opportunities for professional learning.[59] One notable finding is that increased opportunities for participation result in greater conflict.[60] This conflict is related to role ambiguity and increases in workload, something that I follow up on in the next section.

What Barriers Inhibit Teacher Leadership Initiatives?

Experiments with teacher leadership are not always successful.[61] One reason for failure has to do with the ideas and feelings that participants bring to these experiments. Administrators and teachers may have difficulty working outside of the traditional bureaucratic cultures and structures to which they are accustomed. Administrators are not always willing to surrender power to others.[62] But even those who are able to do so find that it is difficult to escape the authority and responsibility that accompanies their position because they will inevitably have to answer for others if things go wrong.[63] Teachers may also not be keen to abandon the comfort of having others make decisions and take responsibility.[64] Teachers are also sometimes reluctant to participate in governance activities, and they may not want to break solidarity with colleagues by assuming authority that their colleagues do not have.[65]

In these unfamiliar situations of teacher leadership, teachers and administrators may not know what their respective roles are or what they should be.[66] Teachers and administrators often have different ideas about what their respective roles should be. This ambiguity generates conflict and anxiety on the part of teachers and administrators.[67] Still, conflict is not just the result of uncertainty about roles; it also emerges as participants move into positions in which they disclose their differences more overtly.[68] But this conflict is not necessarily always a bad thing. It may, for example, provide an impetus for change.

Attempts to implement teacher leadership arrangements face other impediments. Two of these are time and work.[69] Leadership activities require extra work, and this work requires additional time. Not surprisingly, teachers often find that they simply do not have enough time to devote to teaching and to these activities. The traditional time patterns in schools do not always help. Inflexible schedules make it difficult for those who teach to engage in other activities,[70] and teachers tend to resent activities that cut into time that is normally spent on classroom-related activities, particularly if they do not have any apparent effect on what happens in the classroom.[71] Implementing teacher leadership arrangements also becomes more difficult when teachers feel that their opinions are not valued and acted on and when they receive little support or few resources.[72]

What Strategies Work Best in Implementing Teacher Leadership?

Although schools often face difficulties when they attempt to implement teacher leadership, some schools have been able to overcome them. There are many examples of successful or partially successful teacher leadership endeavors, and this is perhaps where the research on teacher leadership is most helpful. Researchers have studied many initiatives of this sort in schools and have documented their successes and failures.

For teacher leadership to succeed, teachers and administrators need to approach changes with certain kinds of attitudes, or it will be difficult, if not impossible, for them to cope with substantial changes. To begin with, principals and teachers must be prepared to share power, and they need to be willing and committed to the new arrangements.[73] The uncertainty that is generally associated with changes of this nature requires the participants to be patient and tolerant.[74] Communication is also important in these scenarios.[75] Those involved need to acquire or develop the skills necessary to collaborate effectively.[76] For this to happen, they need to be open, authentic, and honest with others.[77]

School administrators have a crucial role to play in this process because they have more influence than teachers. One of the key things they must do is learn how to share their legal power with others, shifting their orientation from decision makers to facilitators.[78] Administrators need to be well informed. They need to understand all the new roles and be able to explain them to others.[79] It is also important for administrators to do what they can to shape a school culture that supports teacher leadership.[80] But it is not just building administrators who ought to become involved in these tasks. If teacher leadership initiatives are to succeed, district administrators also must do what they can to support them.[81]

More important than individual administrators in this process are institutional arrangements. Those involved in teacher leadership initiatives need to ensure that their institutions support their initiatives. This means embedding and, as far as possible, formalizing teacher leadership practices in institutions.[82] These practices include the following:

- Decision-making arrangements that give teachers real power[83]

- A locally controlled process that allows teachers to frame a definition of empowerment[84]

- Roles that are clearly specified yet not overly constraining[85]

- A climate that supports risk taking[86]

- Processes for helping participants solve problems and manage conflict[87]

- A mechanism for providing adequate resources[88]

- Schedules that allow teachers the extra time they need to participate in leadership activities[89]

- An ongoing process for educating participants[90]

Those involved in teacher leadership initiatives need help to implement and sustain them. These arrangements will be new to participants, and many will not know what to expect from them or how to deal with the novel situations that inevitably arise. Hence, they will need ongoing professional development that prepares them for issues that may arise and provides them with assistance in handling them. Professional development is most effective when it helps participants understand how to set up and engage in problem-solving and decision-making processes[91] and when it focuses on the interpersonal and communication skills required to deal with the inevitable conflict and uncertainty.[92] Learning should be organized to help teachers and administrators critically reflect on their experiences with teacher leadership and learn from them.[93]

Some professional development approaches work better than others. Those that are locally run and directly relevant to real situations seem to offer teachers and administrators the most useful knowledge.[94] One such initiative was the 2020 School Improvement and Professional Development program in Oregon that provided schools with funds to develop school improvement plans initiated by teacher-led site committees.[95] In this case, organizers of the developmental activities did not provide general training. Instead, they organized their activities to take advantage of teachers' need to solve real problems, seek consensus, and communicate. The school-based professional developers chose problems that arose in the school and adapted their learning activities to help participants deal with these problems. Participants could then apply what they learned directly and immediately to the situations in which they were immersed. This approach allowed professional developers to tailor their efforts to the unique and specific needs of their school.

Teacher leadership initiatives are most likely to succeed when they are implemented gradually.[96] Whether they are introduced as part of a systemwide effort or initiated within individual schools, ideas about these sorts of arrangements ought to be gradually nurtured in ways that garner much-needed local support. Imposition from above without support from below limits the survival chances of teacher leadership endeavors. As support grows, discussion and planning need to take place, and everyone affected should be involved. When plans are in place, schools can begin the incremental adoption of teacher leadership practices.[97] This stage takes time. It involves experimentation, trial and error, and considerable negotiations, even when arrangements are clearly laid out.[98] This is the time when conflict is most likely to surface, so those involved need to be patient as people orient themselves to new situations. In some schools, consensus about roles may begin to emerge as early as the second year,[99] but not all schools are the same, and those involved need to realize that schools spawn different forms of leadership in their own ways and time.[100]

Two Cases of Teacher Leadership

Teacher leadership initiatives are rarely free of problems. Difficulties predictably arise in circumstances in which divisions between teachers and administration are prominent, but they can also emerge in schools in which teacher empowerment is seen as a natural extension of the school's history. These situations are illustrated in the following two cases, which involve schools in the Live Oak County School District that participated in the district-sponsored Shared Decision Making (SDM) project.

Brooksville Elementary School had a recent history of authoritarian leadership and administrator-teacher strife.[101] Located in a relatively stable part of southern Live Oak County, its student enrollment of 625 reflects the population of the county. Many students come from low-income families, and 20 percent are not white. The school has two administrators, thirty-eight teachers, and nineteen noninstructional staff. Most of the administrators, teachers, and staff are white females. Administrator-teacher problems began when the volatile Ms. Baker succeeded a long-serving principal. At the time, she believed it was necessary to exert her authority in order to set things right after inheriting a laissez-faire culture. Ms. Baker had a tendency to issue orders, responding to teacher complaints by saying, "As long as the word *principal* is on my door, I make the decisions." Her attitude, however, alienated a number of teachers, particularly those used to the previous regime. So teachers were naturally skeptical about the possibilities for involving teachers in decision making. Even so, 88 percent of the faculty voted to put forward an application to be a pilot school in the district's Shared Decision Making project. As it turned out, their application was successful.

The school's first step was to form three groups to discuss the meaning of SDM and past resentment and frustrations with the district's flexible guidelines. Next, a core group consisting of an administrator and two faculty and grade chairs met to determine the composition of an SDM council, a representative group of stakeholders who would be the school's decision-making body. By the end of the year, a council had been created, procedures for decision making were in place, and consensus about goals had been achieved. Over the next few months, two problems intervened. The first was the extra time that teachers had to put in. The second was what some staff felt was intimidation on the part of Ms. Baker. Believing that their principal was using SDM as a front to continue her control, many teachers were unwilling to voice their opinions and make decisions. At times, Ms. Baker would veto decisions. One teacher, for example, related, "I'm disillusioned. Faculty are not willing to make decisions any more because we feel threatened and intimidated. . . . When we do feel comfortable enough to make a comment or try a decision she is very critical if she doesn't like it. At lot of times she just blatantly says, 'I won't support that.' I don't speak up at meetings any more. I'd rather give it back to her and let her do it."[102]

The SDM initiative stumbled along for a year or so, turning the corner only after a productive meeting in which, against the wishes of the meeting facilitator, everyone sought to address the problems that plagued the project. At the meeting, the group decided on just one decision-making body, disbanding the three-person core group. In addition, they clarified the roles of individuals and agreed to meet regularly to address communication and increase teachers' input in decision making. In time, the principal made an effort to let others make decisions, although it was difficult to make a decision that Ms. Baker opposed. But teachers also began to understand why Ms. Baker was involved in the way that she was. One teacher commented, "I see the principal coming to us more and more and conferring with us and making it seem as if she wants to decide together, but there are times when it is solely her decision. Some-times it is a matter of time. I understand that; it's not a problem. On important issues, we sit down together."[103] While the school had a long way to go, it had made progress.

Fredericks Middle School found itself in a different position from Brooksville's.[104] It had a long history of administrator-teacher col-laboration, and many believed that shared decision-making arrange-ments were just the next logical step. Fredericks houses 1,500 students in sixth to eighth grade, who are taught by seventy-eight teachers, 13.4 percent of whom are African Americans. The 317 students who are enrolled in the school's special multicultural pro-gram come from fifty-two countries and speak thirty-two languages. The teachers are organized into teams that cover the three grades. Students throughout the district are eligible to attend Fredericks, and the waiting list at the time of the study had 13,000 names. Par-ent involvement is so high that some teachers feel that it increases their workload.

Not surprisingly, 96 percent of the staff voted to apply for par-ticipation in the district's pilot project, despite the fact that the school was undergoing major construction, had recently changed principals, and was in the midst of difficult contract negotiations. Initially, Fredericks developed a plan for deciding how to form the SDM council. This took some time, but in the end, a council was established, and it proceeded to develop a number of school im-provement plans. Progress in integrating shared decision making into the life of the school, however, proved to be slow and more dif-ficult than many at the school had imagined it would be. Fredericks was still experiencing difficulties two and a half years after it had begun the process.

Problems with shared decision making centered on the mean-ing of SDM, the roles of the players, and communication. Teach-ers had different ideas about the purpose and practice of SDM. Many teachers saw it as a process in which they were consulted about problems but were not responsible for developing or implementing solutions. Participants were unclear about their respective roles, leading to conflict over control of decisions in meetings. Communication about these issues was poor; meetings only occurred once a month and lasted for only thirty minutes. Minutes from the meetings were not always distributed, so those who were not at the gatherings did not always know what was going on. Even so, the Fredericks school community was committed to the project, and they consciously addressed the issues, sometimes with the help of a consultant. They met more often and for longer periods of time, organized gatherings to rekindle dwindling enthusiasm for the project, and held meetings in the summer. Eventually, things improved. According to one teacher, "Those of us who attend meetings consistently now understand each other's perspective. [Now] when someone starts talking we don't get angry or offended; we realize where he's coming from, we understand him. I think we're more mature now."[105] Despite this progress, shared decision making was still not integrated smoothly into the working of the school when the research came to an end. Not all teachers were engaged in conversations about shared decision making, and not all were prepared to take responsibility for making decisions.

Summary

The extensive research on teacher leadership has much to offer inclusive leadership by providing useful information about why schools should adopt teacher leadership practices and what they look like. The literature also supplies insight into potential barriers to successful implementation and outlines what needs to be done for teacher leadership to work. On the other hand, the preoccupation of teacher leadership research with influence processes precludes inquiry into leadership goals—in particular, social justice and inclusion issues. Moreover, it focuses on the inclusion of only one group—teachers—and provides little, if any, information on other groups, including students and parents.

Research on teacher leadership has also provided evidence to challenge an individual view of leadership. It suggests that there is a difference in the way some scholars think about leadership and what actually happens in schools and other organizations.[106] Research on teacher leadership has revealed that leadership is not simply a function of an individual leader's ability, knowledge, charisma, and cognition, but is part of a sociocultural context.[107] In other words, influence is more than the product of an individual's actions. Rather, it is best understood as a distributed or organizational practice that encompasses a variety of artifacts, tools, language, people, and relationships.[108] These findings have implications for the practice of leadership and for school improvement. They point to the fact that schools improve not necessarily as a result of individual people doing remarkable things in isolation but as a consequence of a variety of people working together in many different ways and roles, using the multitude of resources that are available to them.[109]

Student Leadership

Student leadership in schools has become more visible in recent years. Once adults who ran schools gave little consideration to student input, but now they are making efforts to include students in many aspects of schooling. Students are having more say in the actual running of schools and in the curriculum and how it is taught. Despite these changes, however, questions remain as to the real impact of this sort of inclusion. Indeed, instances of influential student participation remain few and far between,[110] and in most parts of the Western world, this participation is not embedded in policy.[111] In some instances, initiatives that look to involve students are seen as mere tokenism.

Despite the cynicism in some quarters over student leadership, school systems have in recent years taken steps to introduce mechanisms that allow students to participate in influence processes in schools. These mechanisms include representation on school councils, student councils, school improvement teams, advisory teams, and school boards.[112] Students have also been asked to complete surveys and participate in roundtable discussions; they have had the opportunity to serve on government commissions and school accreditation panels; and they have been part of various student associations and groups.[113]

Students have also had the opportunity, at least in principle, to influence decisions about curriculum content and organization, textbooks, evaluation practices, school rules, discipline, and controversial issues.[114] But these measures do not always ensure real student influence. Student roles of this sort are rarely embedded in policy, and when they are, they are generally advisory in nature. For example, a recent policy initiative in the province of Ontario has made a place for students on local school boards, but only in an advisory capacity.[115]

One reason that student leadership is not more common is that some educators oppose it, believing that students are not capable of making sound educational decisions, lack confidence, cannot handle the heavy workload associated with this sort of involvement, and are only around for a few years.[116] Other educators are put off by young people's tendency to challenge traditions and injustices, a lack of time, heavy teaching loads, tight school schedules, potential conflict between teachers and students, and a lack of knowledge about how to include students in policy processes.[117]

Those who argue in favor of student leadership generally cite three kinds of arguments. First, students have a right to be involved in decisions that affect them. The United Nations Convention on the Rights of the Child recognized that children not only have the right to protection and the right to educational services but also the rights of participation and citizenship. Schools cannot ignore the views of young people just because they are young.[118] Second, student input can improve schools.[119] Students have valuable knowledge of classrooms and school processes that can be used to make schools better places.[120] Students' involvement in determining learning opportunities also increases their motivation to learn. When those involved in the learning process have some input into it, they will be more likely to feel that they belong and become engaged.[121] Finally, students can learn valuable lessons about democracy in schools that actually practice democratic values.[122]

There are a few examples of student leadership initiatives in the literature.[123] One of these describes the Reaching Success through Involvement (RSI) project, which consisted of seventeen schools across the United States that involved students in activities designed to improve the schools.[124] The project began with principals' asking influential faculty to review data about their respective schools' effectiveness; the results of these surveys were used as a baseline for planning. Next, members of these two groups identified formal and informal student leaders and invited them to help plan a retreat. At the two-and-a-half-day retreat, they formed learning teams, set goals to improve their schools, and came up with strategies for recruiting students, faculty, and community members to help with the project. The expanded teams then reviewed goals, developed school improvement plans, implemented solutions, created assessment measures, and used data to plan further activities. The planning teams met in the middle and at the end of the year, then repeated the entire process the following year.

The RSI project generated a number of positive outcomes. Most obvious was improved discipline in all participating schools. Schools reported fewer suspensions, less tardiness, fewer disciplinary referrals, increased daily attendance, and more students participating in school activities. The project increased students' sense of belonging, their perceptions of control over their own education, and their feelings of personal responsibility for the school. The project's activities also taught students how to talk with teachers and helped teachers to talk with rather than at students. But this dialogue did not spill over into classrooms or to other aspects of schooling. Teachers in this study did not encourage students to employ their newly acquired skills in the classroom, and students refrained from attempting to do so. In the end, perceptions of classroom ownership and membership did not change.

The same could not be said of student-educator relationships in School X, a high school in Japan.[125] Established in 1965, this academic elite school of 951 students is located near Tokyo. Most who live in this bedroom community commute daily to the larger city. At the time of the study, the school, students, and teachers believed that their relationship was "more equal" in and out of the classroom than it had been prior to implementing student leadership initiatives. They also believed that students exerted real influence in the school. Indeed, over the years, students were responsible for organizing events like the school graduation and for changing school rules that involved such practices as the dress code and protocols at the graduation ceremony. They were able to do this because they were well organized and hardworking and because their inclusion extended to many aspects of schooling. Their well-supported student council regularly solicited opinions from fellow students through surveys and drop boxes. Students also had a place on the school council, and they did not hesitate to make their positions known to the adults on the council. They felt free to discuss their opinions with teachers, and they sometimes did this in the classroom. One student commented on how natural it feels to voice their opinions: "I feel that it is natural to have a voice because I am used to it at X. Although I wondered if it was okay for me to voice opinions when I first entered here, we can say many things. I now think it is natural for us to have a voice. We would remain passive if we could not have a voice and do anything. I think making school life more pleasant and fruitful includes that students actively voice opinions . . . themselves."[126]

A study by Andy Hargreaves and his colleagues illustrates in more detail how student leadership can extend to the classroom.[127] The twenty-nine teachers from four large school districts in Ontario who were interviewed described how they included students in planning curriculum outcomes and assessing students.

Some teachers simply shared curriculum goals openly and explicitly; others involved students in the curriculum planning process. By involving students in the planning, they were able to test what the curriculum goals meant and how they worked practically. One teacher described the process: "The kids and I go to the wall where the outcomes are written once in a while in our classroom and say, 'Here's what we are doing right now. It fits here.' They can see the connection with outcomes very quickly, and that's fine. The kids are happy with it."[128]

Teachers in the study also involved students in assessment practices by encouraging self-assessment. Students were expected not only to understand their learning but also to take responsibility for it. Teachers motivated students to develop greater independence, set up their own learning plans, identify what they needed to know, and monitor their own learning over time. One teacher promoted self-assessment by getting students to use a chart: "They write the outcome and then they write the activities once they have that related to that outcome. Then they self-assess how they have done on that specific outcome."[129]

The literature on student leadership has provided a number of insights into inclusive leadership. It has shown that there are many ways in which students can become involved in the operation of schools and that there are very good reasons for including students in influence processes. Students should be included for both moral and pragmatic reasons. The arguments behind these justifications outweigh the objections that some educators have to allowing student input. Research has revealed that students are knowledgeable about school processes and that they take the interests of schools to heart.[130] This does not mean that including students in school operations will be easy. Students and educators may not know how to approach student leadership initiatives, and conflict may ensue when they do proceed. One way to deal with this is to involve students, teachers, and administrators in activities that will teach them how to conduct themselves when implementing student leadership initiatives. In the long run, for student leadership to work, it must become part of the normal operations of a school, which means that students' formal participation needs to be included in policy.

Community Involvement

Like student leadership, the idea and practice of including parents in the operation of schools has become more popular over the past few years. Not only have parents been encouraged to venture into their children's schools, but they have also been asked to participate in policy and decision-making processes.[131] Initiatives to include the community in school operations have taken two forms—empowerment and enablement.[132]

Strategies associated with empowerment target what its advocates see as the main problem: the lack of power that various individuals and communities have over educational institutions.[133] The main culprits in this scenario are self-absorbed educational bureaucracies, which seek to retain power for themselves, excluding already powerless parents, particularly those who are poor and those who belong to particular ethnic groups. Ensuring meaningful inclusion, then, requires the empowerment of these otherwise powerless parents. This empowerment will happen only when school systems create alternate structural arrangements that give parents a voice in the governance of educational institutions. These changes would help parents become more satisfied with their children's schools and more committed to education and also help students increase their academic achievement.[134]

The other approach to community inclusion is enablement. Advocates of the enablement perspective do not believe that the cause of exclusion is powerful, self-absorbed, professionally staffed bureaucracies.[135] In some situations, however, some people can have too much power and others too little, and power can sometimes be abused. Bureaucracies can be unresponsive and sometimes dysfunctional, but these power differentials and bureaucratic shortcomings can be resolved from within the system. Thus, the emphasis is not on power per se but on commitment to schools in a rapidly changing social environment. It is up to educational professionals to change themselves and the organizations in which they work to reach out to the community and draw it into the school enterprise. Educators are encouraged to provide incentives for parents to become involved in their children's education for educational rather than political ends. Getting parents to work as resources in their children's education, eliciting their commitment to the educational enterprise, and working out more collaborative arrangements among school, parents, and community will ultimately enhance student achievement.[136]

Not all inclusive school-community proposals or practices turn out to be exclusively of the empowerment or the enablement variety. Some include elements of both, and so-called enablement programs sometimes value empowerment. Perhaps the reforms that follow the empowerment model most closely occurred in large urban American centers in the 1980s and 1990s. Looking for alternatives to systems that had failed the black populations of these areas, various groups in such cities as Philadelphia, Baltimore, New York, Detroit, and Chicago banded together to make changes to what once had been large bureaucratic systems.[137] New legislation paved the way for massive decentralization that allowed local parents a voice in the governance of their children's schools.

Not all urban American centers sponsored empowerment reforms, however. Educational reforms in Miami and Los Angeles followed more of an enablement model. In these cities, insiders rather than outsiders controlled the decentralization process, and as a result, they were able to make changes administratively and control the inclusionary process. Many inclusive school-community reforms in the Western world have combined the two models. In some areas—for example, Ontario—parents remain relatively powerless, even though parental roles have been legislated. In the United

Kingdom, on the other hand, legislation has provided parents with more power than they previously had and, undoubtedly, with more power than Ontario parents currently have. In both cases, though, a strengthening of central powers—for example, the power to control curriculum offerings—has rendered any gains parents have made relatively meaningless.[138]

While enabling tactics and events are important in getting parents—particularly those who are reluctant—involved in school activities, they constitute only a part of inclusive practice. Inclusion goes beyond bake sales, cultural events, parent nights, and the like. Enabling strategies of this sort are designed almost exclusively to help diverse groups adjust to new environments that are very different from those they previously knew. The educators who use such strategies generally take for granted that it is these families and not the school that must change; diverse community groups are expected to acclimatize themselves to practices that do not include their own. While some schools may make valiant efforts to include the languages, cultures, values, and knowledge of the respective community groups in the content and process of schooling, no guarantee can be made that any of this will occur. However, if school knowledge is to be consistently inclusive in the ways that empowerment advocates recommend, power relationships cannot exclusively favor a school system based on Anglo culture. Rather, power relationships must make it possible for community groups to make decisions that will allow school knowledge to be inclusive. If schools are to pay more than lip service to the idea of inclusion, these groups need to be genuinely empowered.

Recent research indicates that the participation of parents in governance does not necessarily ensure that inclusion will occur or that marginalized students will succeed. Studies of school councils in Chicago,[139] Ontario,[140] and the United Kingdom[141] illustrate that even in situations in which parent councils have power over finances, school programs, and personnel, relationships between community and school have not changed all that much[142] and student achievement gains are inconsistent at best.[143] Local community management generally has floundered in three areas: participation on school councils, power on school councils, and the relationship of governance to teaching and learning.

School councils tend to be populated and dominated by Anglo and middle-class parents, and when minority parents do participate, they often have difficulty with the group interaction.[144] In the United Kingdom, this tilt toward Anglo, middle-class parent councils happens because minority parents are not part of the influential informal parent, business, political, and educational networks that generally place individuals on the councils. Asian parents, for example, do not participate on school councils because they lack confidence in their language abilities and in their ability to interact in the white-dominated formal environment of the school. Work commitments and the reluctance of women to go to meetings on their own also account for this low turnout. And when minority parents do participate, they often find that they are unable to penetrate the language and forms of interaction that councils generally adopt.[145]

Those with little experience of formal meetings—including many minority, working-class, and immigrant parents—have difficulty with the procedures of chaired meetings,[146] which some have called "middle-class proceduralism."[147] Not only do many of these parents have to struggle with language barriers, but they also have difficulty with the peculiar type of interaction that this setting engenders and with the informal ways of talking that occur. Thus, they often have difficulty negotiating both formal and informal language situations. These incongruencies routinely obstruct the voices of minority parents and block or filter issues of race.[148] One Philadelphia council member expresses his frustration with the process: "Due to the fact that the participants of the Governance Council are from a very specific situation—all are teachers/administrators, are from the same school, and have been oriented through the years to a particular system and culture—the language, thinking and dialogue left me always playing catch-up ball with such important subjects as meaning of words and concepts, philosophy of education, and contextual questions that relate [to this high school]. This promotes a high level of frustration."[149]

While parents—especially minority and working-class parents—generally do not have the resources or skills to influence governance situations, principals do. Principals have demonstrated a remarkable capacity to either derail community-dominated councils in order to retain decision-making control for themselves or ensure council effectiveness.[150] On the positive side, they can help create participatory decision-making structures and foster collaborative work among council members,[151] clearly define goals and roles for parents and for the council, and act as an information provider, motivator, and friend of the council. On the other hand, principals' unique access to information, their positional power, and their ability to use abstract language to talk about educational issues and to set meeting agendas make it possible for them to smother or exclude individuals and initiatives that do not meet with their approval.[152] When parents do attempt to speak out, their efforts may be undermined. Hyacinth, a mother, community liaison worker, and educator in the African-Caribbean community in an urban environment, says,

> In my school the principal is so dominant that the other poor parents are afraid to speak up. When they do, he speaks in jargon so we can't understand, or ignores us. Because I speak up, they (the principal, vice-principal, and one teacher) gang up on me, or "forget" to tell me when the next meeting is to occur. I find that I have to look on the bulletin boards and call other parents to find out where the meeting is—and I was elected to be part of the council; the other parents don't have much of a voice at all.[153]

Despite such obstacles, a few schools, like La Escuela Fratney in Milwaukee, have made attempts to overcome power imbalances.[154] Saved from extinction by a group of parents and teachers, this school has gone on to become a model of inclusive governance in a racially integrated working-class neighborhood. A site-based management council that consists of parents and teachers makes all the major decisions. For a time, though, after the initial euphoria associated with the school's reopening had dissipated, the council had difficulty attracting members that represented the entire community. Those who continued to be involved were mostly white, middle-class parents who reflected only a small segment of the population. The council took three steps to rectify this situation. First, it established quotas on the council, ensuring that African American and Latino parents had seats. Second, the council redirected funds to hire two part-time parent organizers, a Mexican American and an African American. Finally, with the help of the Wisconsin Writing Project, it paid fifteen parents to participate in a six-week evening workshop in which they discussed school issues and wrote about their children. The purpose of the workshop was to get parents more involved with the school. The council also took measures to alleviate tensions between parents—for example, ensuring that meeting agendas were well planned and that meetings were well run and making it possible for much of the actual work to be done in smaller subcommittees at times and places convenient for the parents.

While schools like La Escuela Fratney have attained a measure of success, they still face many obstacles in their efforts to make education a truly equitable and inclusive enterprise. In some respects, decentralization has masked rather than resolved issues of race and class in inclusionary policies by using the idea of inclusion to give the appearance of change without much resource redistribution; whites maintain their hegemony, while blacks maintain their "control" of public schools. This continuing relationship has made it difficult for parents from marginalized groups to assume a role in governance that they neither wanted nor were prepared for. In addition, decentralization has not had a noticeable impact on student achievement.[155]

Efforts to promote equity in schools may also be frustrated by the efforts of certain parent groups. Take the case of Woodrow Wilson High School, a large, diverse urban school in a politically liberal East Coast American university town.[156] During the 1990s, the school community made a concerted effort to increase the achievement of black and Hispanic students, by taking such measures as reducing the number of curriculum track levels to two and relaxing the entry requirements for most advanced classes. These changes proved positive. After five years, the African American and Hispanic students were more likely to receive college-eligible grades, participate in more rigorous courses, and enroll in universities. These successes were threatened, however, by pressures from the community. Perceiving that the changes favored disadvantaged students at the expense of their own higher-achieving children, a group of mostly white, middle-class parents mobilized to lobby against these reforms. They skillfully used an electronic mail listserv and informal contacts to organize themselves and to move their agenda forward. They were able to convince one of the district administrators who had initially favored the reforms that there were problems with them.

Changes in the relationship between schools and communities will also require changes in society generally. Not only should parents organize and schools and communities be restructured to work toward more democratic arrangements,[157] but everyone needs to work to develop conditions of life that facilitate these inclusive practices. To achieve this end, parents, community members, and educators have to work together. Parents should not be saddled with running schools, nor should they be subordinated to the existing structure. Instead, a model needs to be developed that allows for parents and educators to collaborate on certain parts of children's education.[158] This involvement, however, should not be mandated;

rather, policy should merely set the stage for parents and schools to work together. Such partnerships may require that educators employ the strategies of grassroots organizers to support low-income families and families of color so that they will be better able to be equal participants in schools.[159] Moreover, this collaboration needs to make children's learning a priority. In this regard, it ought to acknowledge the necessity of finding ways to accommodate both professional and nonprofessional commitment and expertise.

Long-term improvement in student achievement will require development of the capacity of professional educators because constraints on the exercise of these capacities will limit improvement of student learning opportunities.[160] But practices geared to improve the professional expertise and commitment of educators cannot be exclusive, as they have traditionally tended to be. Rather, professional teaching practice needs to be inclusive; it must incorporate a range of diverse community knowledge, practices, and values. To ensure that this happens, parents and community members have to play some part in collaborative governance arrangements. Having input into the kind of knowledge that is favored in the classroom and how this knowledge is treated will help to ensure that various, often excluded perspectives are included and validated. Only in this manner can parents, community members, and educators expect to improve learning for all students and to address and alleviate the inequalities that have plagued educational institutions and the conditions of life generally.

The literature on community inclusion provides a number of useful ideas. First, there is value in including parents in the operation of schools. Parents have much to offer schools, and they need to have meaningful opportunities to make these contributions. But their participation needs to go beyond mere enablement roles. For their voices to be heard and their perspectives to be fairly represented in governance and the curriculum, they also need to be genuinely empowered. Getting parents involved in influence processes, however, is not always easy, particularly in cases of immigrant, minority, and working-class parents. Because some members of these groups tend to shy away from governance roles, school councils are usually composed of members of the majority culture. For community inclusion to work, school communities need to work together to ensure that everyone has the opportunity to either participate or be fairly represented in governance processes.

Second, when members of marginalized groups do participate, they frequently find themselves at a disadvantage. They may find it difficult to influence decisions because they have difficulty with the language that people use and the procedures that meetings adopt. People may be excluded from leadership processes for reasons other than those relating to traditional organizational and bureaucratic hierarchies. People regularly are excluded by barriers associated with class, ethnicity, gender, and so on. The sooner that schools and educators recognize this, the sooner they can work to address this issue.

Third, parent, student, and teacher inclusion in governance and influence processes will mean very little if such participation does not find its way into the classroom. Schooling is fundamentally about student learning, and the way in which schools are organized will mean little if at some point their organization does not have an impact on student learning.

Leadership and the Inclusion of Differently Abled Students

The research on leadership and differently abled students is similar to and different from the view of inclusive leadership that I am advocating. It resembles my view in the way that it emphasizes the ultimate ends of the leadership process. All of the literature on inclusion of differently abled students promotes a view of leadership that aims to include all students in the process of formal education. This view of inclusion, however, is more acutely focused than the general view of inclusion that I favor. It emphasizes primarily the prospects of differently abled students rather than all marginalized students.

On the other hand, this view of leadership also highlights the process of leadership. In doing so, though, this largely empirically based body of research promotes a very diverse set of approaches to leadership. While some of these views are inclusive, others are decidedly exclusive. Despite these inconsistencies, this body of literature has much to offer, particularly with regard to the strategies for pursuing the ultimate goals of leadership.

This view of leadership is part of a movement that seeks to include differently abled students in regular schools and classrooms. Originating in Scandinavia and known by different names, such as *mainstreaming* and *integration*, it advocates that differently abled students should not be segregated from so-called normal students. Instead, its central principle is that students with special needs should be integrated into regular classrooms in their local schools.[161] Proponents believe that inclusion should be pursued because differently abled students have more to gain from being educated with regular students than they do from segregated environments,[162] that all students have a right to be educated in regular school settings,[163] and that peers, the school community, and society benefit from these arrangements.[164]

Leadership is the key to successful inclusion programs.[165] Effective leadership can address the many challenges that educators face in creating inclusive environments, such as the extra and sometimes extraordinary efforts required of educators.[166] Educators have to deal with changes in instructional techniques and classroom routines, additional planning efforts and time, accommodating adults in the classroom, and training in the use of medical equipment.[167] Often, they also have to cope with a lack of human and physical resources or a lack of training and support.[168]

Leadership is also needed to deal with negative attitudes toward inclusion. Resistance to inclusion is common. Teachers who are not special education specialists tend to oppose inclusion.[169] Many believe that they are not prepared to receive students with special needs and that inclusive environments will bring on extra work and stress for them.[170] But teachers are not the only ones who do not support inclusion. Administrators are also sometimes hesitant to endorse the principle of inclusion,[171] and when they do, their support is often qualified. Most principals are pragmatic, and given the opportunity, they will evaluate students for inclusion on a case-by-case basis, even when they express support of inclusion of all students.[172] This is significant because the success or failure of inclusion efforts in schools will depend, to some extent, on the beliefs and actions of administrators.[173]

Obviously, leadership practices espoused by proponents of inclusion of the differently abled champion the attainment of inclusion. They focus exclusively on efforts to mobilize support for inclusion, implement inclusive practices, and monitor efforts. Given the challenges of inclusion and the resistance to it, however, much text is devoted to garnering support for inclusion. The leadership approaches that are recommended for obtaining support for inclusion range from transformational, individualistic practices to emancipatory, collective processes. Researchers who favor transformational leadership do so because they believe the behaviors associated with it represent the best chance of marshaling support for inclusive ideals and practices.[174] More specifically, they feel that charismatic leaders stand the best chance of motivating teachers to go beyond the call of duty, which in this case would include supporting inclusion and doing the extra things that need to be done in inclusive classrooms.[175] Emancipatory proponents, on the other hand, maintain that support for inclusion can come only through dialogue and inquiry over a period of time.[176]

Regardless of philosophy or allegiance, the literature has many suggestions for garnering support for inclusion, including the following:

- Making inclusion a nonnegotiable reality[177]

- Sharing with others the theoretical, ethical, and research-based rationales for inclusive education[178]

- Involving school and community stakeholder groups in formulating objectives for schooling that supports all students[179]

- Creating cognitive dissonance and discomfort in regard to exclusive practices and a sense of urgency about inclusion[180]

I elaborate on these ideas in Chapter Four.

Research indicates that educators need to believe in inclusion in order for it to succeed in schools. But this is not enough. Leadership practices also have to embed this belief and the related practices in the culture and structure of schools.[181] Ideally, schools need to develop a culture and esprit de corps that embraces the values and practices of inclusive education.[182] To do this, teachers need support in the form of physical and human resources and support for critiquing systems of inclusion in order to improve them, for making their own decisions, for solving their own problems, and for taking risks.[183] Teachers and administrators must be provided with in-service programs that address issues in conflict resolution, staffing management, problem solving, collaborative decision making, student discipline, relationships with parents, and instruction and curriculum in inclusive environments.[184] Finally, inclusive practices need to be monitored.[185]

Woodland Hills, an elementary school in a medium-sized midwestern metropolitan school district, displays some of the characteristics of a successful program of inclusion.[186] The 480 students who attend classes display a variety of disabilities and ethnicities, and a high percentage belong to low socioeconomic and highly mobile groups. Many of the school's inclusive practices were initiated by Marta, the principal, who began her teaching career as a special education teacher. Like Mr. G, who was described earlier in this chapter, she provided a supportive environment for critique. Marta let teachers make instructional decisions, shifted problem solving to them, communicated trust, encouraged risk taking, and modeled inquiry. One third-grade teacher was particularly grateful for the support she received when she experimented:

> I have felt really supported in some experimentation that I wanted to try like I remember saying to Marta on more than one occasion, "It's so nice to work with somebody who has an idea about what I'm trying to do with kids." She is willing to look at the overall picture rather than trying to make me fit some type of mold. . . . I've tried all kinds of things. . . . When you have all kinds of kids in your class, you just have to try more than one thing, and she is more interested in knowing how things turn out than anything else.[187]

But unlike Mr. G., Marta initiated these strategies to achieve a very particular goal—inclusion. While critique of procedures was encouraged, the goal of inclusion of students with disabilities in general education classrooms was not open to critique. Marta describes one episode in which she confronted a teacher who talked about inclusion in a derisive manner: "A teacher came up to me and said, 'Did you know that _____ is calling inclusion "intrusion"?' I said, 'How interesting.' I went down to talk with this woman, told her that I had heard she called inclusion intrusion. Well, naturally she was a bit flustered. She replied, 'Oh, that was just a joke.' I told her, 'We don't make jokes about kids' lives.'"[188]

Marta also brought spiritual elements to her leadership that influenced her other practices. These included the value of personal struggle, the dignity of the individual, a fusion of professional and personal values and practices, a trust in people, and the importance of listening and dreams. Marta describes her listening ability, which, she maintains, grew out of her spirituality: "I learned to value people, I learned not to interrupt, which is such an important part of leadership. I learned to be available for people. I am much more available to people than I used to be. When I talk with people, I really listen, I am there with them. I . . . feel like . . . my spiritual groundedness has helped me . . . to have an agenda."[189]

While the school accomplished many important goals, the problem with this form of leadership was that Marta occupied a prominent role. Like Mr. G.'s and Jim Laughton's schools, Woodland Hills' inclusion policies face an uncertain future when she departs.

Research on inclusion of differently abled students has provided much useful information about leadership and inclusion. Like other approaches, though, it has drawbacks. For example, researchers in this area promote a variety of very different and often inconsistent approaches to leadership processes. Some, like emancipatory leadership, are compatible with inclusion, but others, such as transformational leadership, are not. The most valuable contribution of this literature to inclusive leadership is in indicating how to pursue the ultimate goals of leadership. Researchers who are interested in inclusion of the differently abled are preoccupied with achieving particular goals, and they believe that leadership efforts are key to attaining them. These ends, however, are somewhat narrower in scope than the inclusive ideals favored in this book. Even so, those interested in promoting more general inclusive ends have much to learn from the manner in which goals are emphasized and pursued by champions of students with special needs.

Proponents of a more general approach to inclusion must acknowledge the inevitable resistance to inclusion. Many will oppose initiatives for more inclusive processes in regard to gender, class, and race. This resistance will come not just from overtly sexist, racist, and homophobic individuals but also from supporters of gender, class, and race rights who take for granted the subtle privileges that they enjoy from their membership in certain groups. It is important for leadership processes to acknowledge this resistance and to find ways to advocate for inclusive ideals and practices. In this sense, leadership approaches to the differently abled can offer an important contribution to inclusive leadership.

Conclusion

The literature on various types of inclusive leadership has been useful in sketching out what inclusive leadership should look like and in providing suggestions about how interested parties might proceed in promoting and implementing it. Most important, it gives us an idea of how leadership arrangements might be organized and implemented and how they might work for inclusion generally. Among other things, those interested in putting inclusive leadership into practice need to consider how to

- Think about leadership
- Include participants
- Advocate for inclusion
- Educate participants
- Develop critical consciousness
- Promote dialogue
- Emphasize student learning and classroom practice
- Adopt decision-making and policymaking practices
- Incorporate whole-school approaches

The next chapter elaborates on these themes.

4

Making Inclusive Leadership Work

This chapter provides practical suggestions for promoting and implementing inclusive leadership. These propositions should be seen as part of a flexible framework for approaching inclusive leadership, not as ingredients of a magic formula or as rigid prescriptions. Readers need to consider these proposals and, where appropriate, tailor them for the unique contexts in which they are working.

Thinking About Leadership

We need to change the way that we think about leadership. To be consistent with the ideals of inclusive leadership, we must move away from seeing leadership, as many do, in terms of individuals and as a form of hierarchy among people. This view sees leadership as embodied in individuals. It presumes that single, often heroic, individuals are capable of influencing others in ways that make their organizations and institutions better places.[1] This popular view of leadership also favors hierarchical relationships that distinguish leaders from followers. This type of arrangement allows the allegedly more skilled and powerful leaders to control, motivate, and organize the less talented and powerful followers to help the organization achieve its goals. Supposedly, followers need others to tell them what to do because they cannot be trusted to perform tasks on their own. This remains a popular view, despite evidence that points to the efficacy of other arrangements.[2]

Neither the embodiment of leadership in a single individual nor the hierarchical distinction of leaders and followers is consistent with ideals of inclusive leadership. When an individual is awarded the title of leader, others are, by default, deemed to be followers and are excluded from leadership roles and activities. Followers do not have as many opportunities to influence the course of events in organizations; they are expected to abide by the norms established by others. For leadership to be inclusive, everyone needs to have the opportunity to influence what happens in organizations.

Not only are individualistic approaches to leadership exclusive, but they are much less effective than collective practices. Indeed, recent inquiry into leadership makes a case for thinking of leadership as a collective rather than an individual process. Researchers have begun to champion the idea of leadership as something that transcends the actions or effects of individuals. Their studies show that leadership, understood as a social influence process, is not just a function of what particular people in leadership positions know and do.[3] While individuals do matter, they are not all that matters. Leadership is an organizational quality that goes beyond individuals in positions of power; it is distributed across individuals and the contexts in which they interact, intertwined with such things as language, theories in action, interpretive schemas, organizational structures, and various material resources.[4] Thus, schools will improve not as the result of a few individuals doing remarkable things but as the consequence of a variety of people working together in many different ways and roles, using a multitude of resources available to them.[5]

Members of school communities work best together when they are not separated by hierarchy. Only then can the contributions of people with different skills and perspectives be truly honored and factored into school practices. This happens when no single individual or group of individuals is featured or relied on more than others. Thus, it is important to see leadership as a process that transcends the individuals who are a part of it. We have seen, most notably in the case of Jim Laughton in Chapter Three, that in the long run, too heavy a reliance on particular individuals will defeat efforts to make changes. The changes that Laughton made over the course of his fifteen-year tenure were rolled back only a few years after his death. The practices that he championed were not sufficiently entrenched in a process that would have enabled them to survive the loss of his energy, drive, knowledge, and personality. This phenomenon is not unique to Richmond Road School, however; it occurs regularly in schools. Andy Hargreaves, for example, writes about the carousel of leadership succession. His study of principal succession indicates that "principal rotation and repeated successions don't push schools along an upward curve of improvement but around a perpetual carousel in which all of them move up and down with depressing regularity."[6]

Including Members of the School Community

Inclusive leadership approaches include all members of the school community in influence processes. Students, teachers, and parents all have the right to be part of these processes. Ideally, they will have the opportunity to participate in genuine democratic arrangements and will not be subjected to autocratic hierarchies. Some forms of organization favor practices that fall somewhere between these two poles, such as consulting with stakeholders and soliciting various kinds of input. Students, parents, and teachers can also take different roles in leadership processes—some formal, others informal. The respective dispositions, skills, and positions of parents, students, and teachers will dictate that they be included in different ways and at different times. Finally, there are many areas of school practice that various members of the school community can influence. These include teaching-oriented matters such as instruction and curriculum and school-level administrative issues such as budget.

Members of school communities can be included in leadership processes in many ways. Figures 4.1, 4.2, and 4.3 capture the range of potential involvement for teachers, students, and parents. The three dimensions represent levels of potential involvement, associated roles, and possible areas of participation. The levels run from inclusive to

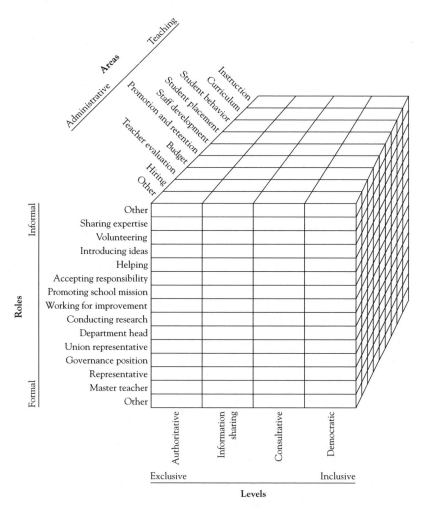

Figure 4.1. Teacher Involvement in Leadership

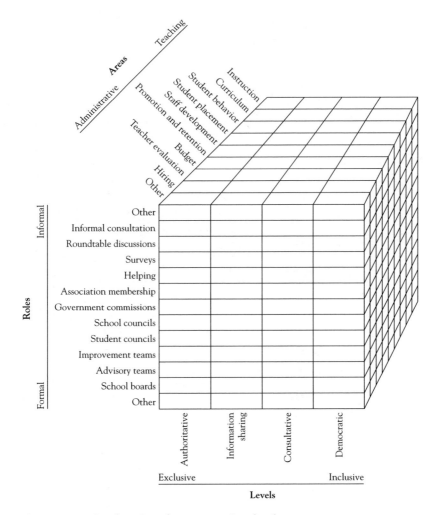

Figure 4.2. Student Involvement in Leadership

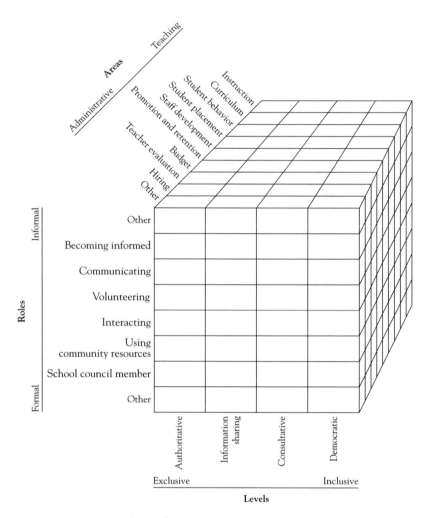

Figure 4.3. Parental Involvement in Leadership

exclusive; roles graduate from informal to formal; and areas range from teaching issues to school-level administrative matters.

Not all groups in school communities, as we have seen, will be in favor of including its members in this way; therefore, leadership activities will have to be organized to advocate for inclusion.

Advocating for Inclusion

Leadership practices need to be organized to promote inclusion because we live in a world that increasingly embraces values, views, and practices that are not consistent with inclusion. These show up in schools and in the world beyond schools. Teachers and administrators are often opposed to the inclusion of differently abled students in mainstream education,[7] but resistance to inclusion extends far beyond this issue. Research indicates that administrators are reluctant to admit to the presence of racism in their schools and that some teachers condone sexism.[8] Some of these exclusive views and practices are obvious, as in cases of blatant racial prejudice; others are subtler and find expression in practices such as testing.

To combat various forms of resistance to inclusion, those involved in leadership enterprises need to be prepared to actively promote inclusion. They need to foster a process that allows them to create and communicate a compelling picture of an inclusive future and to persuade others to commit to that future.[9] Individuals cannot do this alone. Promoting inclusion will require that people forge affiliations with like-minded others with whom they can work to spread the word. People will find it easier to persuade others to recognize and accept the value of inclusion when this belief is embedded in the culture and structure of schools.[10] Strategies that can help this process along include the following:

Make inclusion a nonnegotiable reality.[11] This is not necessarily the best tactic. It is preferable for people to accept the value of inclusion on their own, but it might be necessary to insist on it in cases in which people are not prepared to listen to reason. Marta, who is described in Chapter Three, adopted this strategy.[12] While she was open to the varied forms that inclusion may take, she found it best not to tolerate objections to the principle itself.[13] While this tactic many get some people to conform in their use of inclusive practices, it violates inclusive principles, and it runs of the risk of stoking the fires of resistance.

Create cognitive dissonance and discomfort in regard to exclusive practices and a sense of urgency about inclusion.[14] The preferred strategy is for people to embrace inclusion on their own, without being forced. In reality, however, people may need a stimulus to prompt them out of their comfort with the status quo and lethargy about changing unjust practices. Proponents of inclusion may need to induce a degree of cognitive dissonance that will cause others to question the current state of affairs and look for new and better ways of educating children and promoting inclusion. Strategies for accomplishing this are similar to those employed to promote critical consciousness, which are explained later in this chapter.

Share with others the theoretical, ethical, and research-based rationales for inclusive education and leadership.[15] One of the keys to convincing people of the value of inclusion is providing them with compelling arguments. Evidence from research can help make these cases. If proponents of inclusion want to ensure that others embrace their rationales, they need to be familiar with research on inclusion in general and on specific educational issues that are affected by inclusion or the lack of it.

Trade and bargain.[16] Convincing others to support inclusion may require that school communities do more than present logical or lucid arguments; they may have to bargain with some individuals, groups, and agencies to achieve their goals. School communities will have resources that they can trade for concessions from others, and they should not hesitate to put them to good use. Getting others on board with inclusion may involve this sort of hard bargaining.

Stall and maneuver.[17] Stalling can be a useful technique for both promoting inclusion and resisting exclusion. This tactic may be useful, for example, when school communities are confronted with practices or policies that are obviously or subtly exclusive, like standardized testing. Delaying can give those involved time to plan their actions and to mount campaigns to resist such practices. It will also give them time to consider alternative paths and explore other options.

Establish links between educators and disadvantaged groups.[18] Resistance to equity initiatives on the part of community groups is common. Middle-class parents, for example, have been known to oppose inclusive initiatives. To counter the skillful efforts of such parents, educators will need to link with and support low-income families and families of color by adopting strategies associated with social movements—for example, creating networks that can sustain an activist community, framing a story about the network's identity and purpose, or developing a program that mobilizes and expends resources to advance the group's objectives.[19]

Involve school and community stakeholder groups in formulating objectives for schooling that support all students.[20] An important element in sponsoring successful implementation of inclusive practices is to involve key stakeholders in initial discussions; their support will be crucial to the outcome. They must have the opportunity to air their concerns and to be assured that their worst fears will not come true. It is also useful to involve as many community groups as possible. These may include professional associations, businesses, heritage and religious groups, and community-oriented agencies. Venues available in which proponents of inclusion can talk up their vision include the following:

- Ongoing in-service workshops
- Distribution of readings and follow-up discussions at meetings
- One-on-one dialogues

- Community forums

- Showings of videotapes of inclusive schools

- Visits to inclusive schools[21]

One example of advocating for inclusion occurred at Richmond Road School. Its main instigator was the head teacher, Jim Laughton. To begin with, he believed deeply in inclusion and social justice and he had the ability to articulate this vision in a practical and coherent fashion. His advocacy strategy involved both informal and formal discussions of the ideas associated with this vision. Whenever the opportunity arose, he talked to individual teachers about it, and he also organized weekly discussions at staff meetings. These interactions had a noticeable impact on the school community. One of his teachers, for example, maintained that "given the opportunity to talk with him and listen to him for long enough, you actually improved your own ability to articulate the . . . issues."[22] But as I mentioned earlier, the problem with the scenario at Richmond Road School was that it was too much of a one-man show. Generally the persuasion was being done by Jim Laughton as opposed to it being facilitated by the school's structure or culture. For advocacy of this sort to be effective, it needs to be a collective enterprise; many members of the school community need to be actively engaged in promoting inclusion. This engagement needs an environment or culture that enables and nurtures it.

One of the ways in which inclusion can be promoted is through education.

Educating Participants

Administrators, teachers, students, and parents generally know too little about one another, about exclusive processes like racism, and about how to approach and implement inclusive practices.[23] For everyone to meet the challenges associated with inclusion, they will need to acquire new knowledge, understandings, and attitudes. To do so, all members of the school community have to assume the roles of both teacher and learner. They need to learn about exclusion and inclusion, just as they need to learn about the other members of the educational enterprise. Educators must help parents and students learn about the school system and community and about existing opportunities, and students and parents need to help educators learn about students and their communities. But learning new things and adopting new or different attitudes is not always easy. Accounts of formal attempts to nurture inclusive ideals show mixed results.[24]

Educators can do many things to learn about inclusion-related issues and to teach their communities about them. Many concede, though, that they learn best informally—that is, on the job, through experience in their schools, from their colleagues, from community members, and, less often, from so-called experts at their central office and elsewhere.[25] For administrators, there is often little choice other than informal learning, since few training opportunities are available in the area of inclusion. Administrators also value informal learning over formal training. Nevertheless, some refer to helpful learning experiences associated with workshops and conferences. For these to be helpful, though, they must connect directly with administrators' everyday experiences. University programs that attempt to make such connections for administrators are scarce. The programs that do make such connections feature in-depth fieldwork, internships, and real-life situations that link learners with a wide range of diverse situations.[26]

School-based programs that integrate experience and learning can also be effective. Take the 2020 School Improvement and Professional Development program in Oregon, which is described in Chapter Three.[27] The new responsibilities that teachers acquired generated a need for new knowledge and concrete reasons to solve problems, seek consensus, and communicate. Learning opportunities were then designed to address these particular needs. For example, training in group skills could be applied immediately to real situations that had meaning and value for the participants. Teachers had the opportunity to immediately try out what they had learned in the sessions in their actual practice.

Administrators also feel that there are strategies that they can use to educate their school communities.[28] One of these is modeling. Modeling ideal practices can have a significant impact on students, teachers, and parents. In addition, activities can be designed to educate the school community. Of these, administrators tend to believe that local or school-based sessions are of greater benefit than larger ones. The most learning occurs when avenues are provided for teachers and community members to share their respective areas of expertise with one another. Teachers and parents learn most when they can apply what they learn to their experiences in and out of school.

Attempts have been made to link formal learning situations to the everyday lives of educators by designing ongoing series of meetings and activities.[29] These efforts have not always been successful, however. A two-year staff development program studied by Christine Sleeter, for example, had a limited impact on teachers' ability to deliver multicultural education.[30] Program constraints, the demands of the teaching profession generally, and limited support from others, particularly administrators, made it difficult even for those who were committed to making changes in their respective schools. Not all programs of this sort report negative outcomes, though; it is more likely that they will achieve mixed results.

Lorayne Robertson found that mixed outcomes resulted from the equity development initiative that she studied.[31] Ninety-nine educators participated in in-service sessions on equity issues over a two-year period, taking the information back to follow-up sessions at the school level. Although the majority of participants in the district-wide sessions did change their views, those who held the most extreme (and negative) stances at the school level proved the most resistant to change and, in some cases, engineered forms of backlash against the initiatives. In schools, some areas were more amenable to change than others. School climate, for example, was easier to influence than curriculum.

Recent research has been instructive in regard to countering resistance. It points to the need for less confrontational approaches. A good example of this need is in efforts to combat racism in the United Kingdom.[32] The murder of an Asian student at a school in Manchester prompted those concerned about diversity and inclusion to reassess their approaches to countering racism, particularly the hard line taken by some proponents of racial justice. David Gillborn observed this confrontational approach when he studied two schools. He found that participants in in-service sessions felt that they were being told, "You are racist. You are this." The tactics that proponents of antiracism were using at the time left no room for people to make mistakes or to think about those mistakes. The result was that they generated uncertainty and fear on the part of white teachers. Many felt that they had to think about everything they said and did because they believed there was always a chance that their actions would be interpreted in a way that could lead to their being accused of racism. These tactics tended to reinforce the guilt of many well-meaning whites, paralyzing them when issues of race arose. Others simply buried their racism without changing their attitude. In the end, it created resentment and anger and put an end to free discussion about related issues.

Some educators in Gillborn's study took a more forgiving stance. One of these individuals maintained that simple confrontation was unlikely to succeed. While this teacher said that stereotypes and racist assumptions needed to be routinely challenged, she believed that this was best done within a relationship that already existed. She said, "You don't change people by criticizing them in the beginning. You need to make them think otherwise. And when they come back to you and say 'Oh right, this is how we do it. Oh gosh, when we first came how naïve I was.' "[33]

Schools need to find a balance that maintains pressure to be reflective about current assumptions and practices without being confrontational in a way that merely reproduces and amplifies current conflicts. The best route to take, then, is one that is positive without allowing people to be too comfortable with themselves and that prompts them to reflect on the present state of affairs but doesn't produce the fear and guilt that trigger further conflict. This strategy recognizes that people make mistakes and that these mistakes should be acknowledged and discussed in a constructive manner.

One recent approach to learning has potential for educating not just individuals but whole school communities about inclusion in an organized and enduring manner. This movement has come to be known as *organizational learning*.[34] Peter Senge's disciplines of personal mastery, shared vision, mental models, team learning, and systems thinking, if employed in appropriate ways, can make it possible for school communities to pursue collective, persistent, and critical learning. Learning organizations of the sort that Senge envisions emphasize personal development, mutual purpose, critical reflection, collective learning, dialogue and interaction, and systems thinking—practices consistent with inclusion. Such practices allow all members of school communities to have their respective cultures honored and incorporated into the learning experience, to have a say in the nature of that learning experience, and to have the opportunity to critically examine and eventually challenge systemic forms of exclusion. These practices make it possible for school communities to adjust to the perpetually changing conditions that characterize contemporary communities.

Blue Mountain School, cited in Chapter One, is a good example of how organizational learning can promote inclusion.[35] Envisioned by a pioneering principal who was an advocate of Senge's ideas and supported by a district with a history of opening innovative schools, Blue Mountain developed over time as a learning organization and a professional learning community. The first principal was appointed three years before the school opened, and during that interval, he worked with the architect, local community, and teachers to develop a shared vision that emphasized a student-centered community of care based on strong relationships, mutual respect, and the importance of family. The school was designed to encourage social interaction between teachers and students, and it was equipped with technology to support this desired communication. Structures were put in place to ensure the endurance of this vision beyond the tenure of the first principal and to support personal and collective learning. Leadership was distributed throughout the school in a number of cross-departmental teams that included student representatives and that had responsibility for problem solving, planning, and decision making. The prominence of systems thinking, dialogue, and deep learning helped everyone to see the big picture and to be more aware of the consequences of their actions. One teacher, for example, stated, "Because it's a systems school . . . it works much better for students and for staff because we're not out of the loop. We know what's going on. . . . We're aware of the building and it makes a huge difference, where in my old school I only knew what was happening in my department. . . . So it makes a big difference when the organization of the school is different. And this organization fits my approach to teaching far better."[36]

Collective learning about inclusion issues is important, but this learning also needs to be critical.

Developing Critical Consciousness

Educating the whole school community is important. Also vital, though, is the kind of education in which administrators, teachers, students, and parents participate in critiquing the process. For inclusion to become a normal part of school practices, education needs to be critical in its approach. School communities need to develop a critical consciousness in their members. Ideally, those who acquire this critical consciousness will possess both the skills and the desire to engage in constructive criticism. They will also know enough to direct their critique at a very particular object—their social circumstances.

Being critical means becoming more skeptical about established truths. Being critical requires skills that allow one to discern the basis of claims, the assumptions underlying assertions, and the interests that motivate people to promote certain positions. These skills enable people to scrutinize the evidence and the logic that proponents of a course of action employ to support their arguments and conclusions. Critical skills allow people to recognize unstated, implicit, and subtle points of view and the often invisible or taken-for-granted conditions that provide the basis for these stances. But critical consciousness involves more than just a set of intellectual skills. It also includes an eagerness to engage in this sort of critique and a willingness to follow through on positions. People who possess a critical consciousness have a desire not only to engage in critique but also to act in support of their views.

In inclusive school communities, critique needs to be directed first at the social environment—the school itself and its local and wider communities. Exclusive practices are not always easy to identify, however, because they are often so ingrained in daily life that some educators do not pay much attention to them. Not only are such educators blind to color issues, but they may also display class and spiritual blindness.[37] While some simply cannot recognize differences, others ignore them because they believe that this is the right thing to do. Nothing could be further from the truth. Recognizing, acknowledging, and critiquing taken-for-granted patterns is necessary to turn things around for those who are routinely excluded.

Developing a critical consciousness requires that school communities reflect on their ideas and practices. Members explore not only community and school patterns of exclusion but also their own roles in these patterns. They need to do this because they may be unwittingly playing a part in sustaining and spreading these practices. When people reflect, they consciously attempt to pause, step back from their daily routines, and inquire into their own and others' thoughts and actions.[38] This occurs most often when something unexpected or unusual occurs.[39] Unfortunately, the nature of educators' work does not lend itself naturally to reflection; the hurried pace of the day leaves little space for such a practice. Thus, for school communities to engage in reflection, they must find ways to build opportunities for it into their daily routines.

Critical reflection is a social activity,[40] not just an act of individuals' looking at their private self. Critical reflection is social in two senses. First, it critiques social arrangements, and second, this critique necessarily occurs within these same social arrangements. This presents a dilemma for critical thinkers. They need to be able to think in new and different ways, but the very social environment that they are looking to critique and change provides them with the resources (for example, language, understandings) for the critique. For critical reflection to overcome this limitation, it must go beyond individual introspection. For individuals to break out of their usual, taken-for-granted patterns of thinking, which can obscure exclusion, they need to engage others—particularly different others— in critical conversations. Such critical conversations can help school communities acknowledge, recognize, critique, and change invisible practices that impede inclusion.

An example from one of my studies illustrates the value of engaging in critique with others. Gary, the principal of a large and diverse high school, had always believed that he was very enlightened about diversity issues. Never in his wildest dreams would he have considered himself to be a racist. Gary's belief that he treated everyone the same was shattered, however, during a frank exchange with one of his fellow administrators:

> [You may be thinking,] "I'm not a racist. I'm very liberal and so I don't have a problem with all of these people coming in." You'd better step back because that's

probably not true. We believe that there are all sorts of hidden things that we do in dealing with races different than us and we've got to be cognizant of them. And in admin we tell each other if it happens: "Hey I saw you talking to that kid, your body language was such and such." . . . One of the principals in a meeting said to me, "Have you noticed the difference in the way you talk to Hong Kong families as opposed to South African families?" I said, "There's no difference. I treat everyone the same." "No," he said, "when a Hong Kong family comes in, and there's the mother and father and about eight kids, an auntie who's going to speak for them because none of them speak English, . . . you're not always as warm and wonderful as you should be and you're sometimes patronizing." . . . And my instincts say, "No. That's not true. I don't do that." But I do and I believe everybody does. You don't need to be a racist to have some shifts in the way you act toward people. And so we act as windows for each other and say, "Hey. Wait a minute. Here's what I saw."[41]

School communities can do a number of things to promote critical conversations. First, they can provide an atmosphere that supports critique. It will be easier for everyone to look critically at school and community practices if it is the norm—that is, part of the school's culture. Members of the school community can also engage in activities that are designed to help critical reflection, such as testing out platforms or ideas with diverse others before acting on them; modeling; maintaining administrative portfolios that contain such things as accounts of committees chaired and policies written; keeping journals; examining case records and studies; performing two-column analyses that involve comparing such things as desired outcomes versus actual outcomes; employing various scenario analyses; and participating in simulations and value audits.[42] Employing the arts or using "jujitsu techniques" are other ways to move critical conversations along by helping people see things in different ways. Jujitsu techniques involve reversing ordinary or accepted ways of seeing things.[43] The short Australian film *Babakiueria* illustrates this technique by reversing the positions of Europeans and Aborigines; in the film, Aborigines establish colonies among Europeans. In the process, the Aborigines impose their values and practices on the unsuspecting and generally compliant Europeans. The film makes strange both the cultural practices of the Europeans and the ways of making sense of them. By forcing European viewers to identify with the oppressed people, the film prompts them to take a critical and perhaps alternate view of the process and effects of colonization. Artistic works in other media can also prompt educators to step back from the daily press of life and look at it in new and different ways.[44]

School communities can also structure critical conversations by using sets of questions. For example, Richard Bates has formulated a set of key questions that focus on the kind of knowledge that schools favor:[45]

- What counts as knowledge?

- How is what counts as knowledge organized?

- How is what counts as knowledge transmitted?

- How is access to what counts as knowledge determined?

- What are the processes of control?

- What ideological appeals justify the system?

Other sets of questions include more general questions about the school and the community:

- What is happening here?

- What do we know about this?

- Who says that this is the way things should be?

- What overall purposes are being served?

- Whose vision is it?

- Whose interests are being served?

- Whose needs are being met?

- Whose voices are being silenced, excluded, or denied?

- How come some viewpoints always get heard?

- Why is this particular initiative occurring now?

- What prudent and feasible action can we adopt?

- Who can we enlist to support us?

- How can we start now?

- How are we going to know when we make a difference?[46]

Critical conversations proceed best when these questions are integrated into both classroom and schoolwide activities. La Escuela Fratney, referred to in Chapter Three, promotes a number of school-wide programs in critical thinking skills as part of its commitment to encouraging children to think deeply about the world and to helping them develop their ability to criticize society and their role in it.[47] One such program is "no TV week." Initially, the goal of the program was to wean students off television by getting them to pledge not to watch it for a week. The school changed direction, however, after the first year. It decided that it would be better to teach children to view media critically than to simply try to get them to reduce their television viewing, because most would continue to watch, regardless of their one-week abstinence. Teachers sponsored several projects to develop critical thinking skills. In one second-grade class, the teacher asked her class to examine the kinds of people who are held up as models in society. Making huge murals out of clipped magazine advertisements allowed the students to identify racial bias, gender stereotyping, and an absence of over-weight and bespectacled people. A group of teachers used the show "Teenage Mutant Ninja Turtles" and the accompanying advertise-ments to explore the treatment of violence. This program for devel-oping critical skills has continued, with modifications, over the years. Students and their parents sign no-TV contracts, keep logs of their television viewing habits, write diaries about their week, interview family members about the impact of television on their lives, and examine stereotypes and advertisements.

Promoting Dialogue

Critical conversations work best when schools make an effort to pro-mote dialogue. For school communities to promote critical con-sciousness and inclusive communities generally, they need to nurture dialogue.[48] For everyone to be meaningfully included, schools need to provide opportunities for people to communicate effectively with one another. For these dialogues to succeed, however, participants need to have an emotional investment in them; they have to want to participate in dialogues.[49] It will be easier for people to do this when they are able to trust others. Where there is an element of risk, participants have to know that they can rely on someone or some-thing. Besides trust, other feelings like respect, appreciation, affec-tion, and hope can play an important part in broadening and extending dialogues.

An important aspect of inclusive dialogue is a willingness to listen to everyone in the school community, to make sure that everyone has a voice. Including everyone's voice will help the school community work toward achieving the difficult goals of understanding and consensus. This does not mean, however, that consensus is always possible. But giving everyone a voice represents a starting point for grasping others' points of view and helps to publicly identify institutional barriers that inhibit understanding and consensus.[50] For this to happen, though, certain conditions must be present. Everyone must have an equal opportunity to speak and must respect other members' right to speak out and to feel safe to talk; all ideas must be tolerated and subjected to fair assessment. Some scholars have spent considerable time and effort on schemes of this sort. Jürgen Habermas, for example, calls his approach an ideal speech situation.[51] For public dialogues to work, the settings must allow the dialogues to be comprehensive, truthful, sincere, and correct. Each participant must have an equal opportunity to initiate and continue the conversation, to make assertions and recommendations, and to explain his or her wishes, feelings, and desires.

There are many techniques that participants in dialogue can employ to aid them in listening to others. For example, listeners can establish eye contact (while keeping in mind that eye contact might not be appropriate in some situations, depending on the cultural background of the participants) and take up an appropriate distance from the speaker (which also may vary, depending on the cultures involved). Listeners may also want to avoid interrupting the speaker, compare the speaker's experience with their own, and ask questions.[52] When dominant and nondominant individuals and groups are engaged in dialogue, it is important for listeners from dominant groups to help participants from nondominant groups feel as comfortable as possible in order to help them speak their mind.[53] In these circumstances, participants from dominant groups need to abandon as far as possible any power or influence that they may have in the situation. This may require taking some of the following actions:

- Displacing themselves as knowers and evaluators

- Abandoning a desire to overtly assign a relative worth to observations

- Reflecting on their privileges

- Suspending personal authority

- Being willing to experience vulnerability and to admit ignorance

Effective dialoguing may also require that someone from the dominant group temporarily abandon his or her identity, because, as Lisa Delpit tells us, "Listening requires not only open eyes and ears, but open hearts and minds. . . . To put our beliefs on hold is to cease to exist as ourselves for a moment and that is not easy. It is painful as well, because it means turning yourself inside out, giving up your sense of who you are, and being willing to see yourself in the unflattering light of another's gaze."[54] For administrators and teachers, this may mean stepping outside their role as an authority.

School communities can take specific measures to work toward open dialogues. To begin with, educators can lay the groundwork for fostering relationships with those in their communities by placing themselves in positions that bring them into contact with others—for example, by

- Spending time on the phone for positive reasons

- Making themselves easily available to community members

- Frequenting areas where colleagues, students, and parents gather

- Going out into the community to meet and visit with people

- Exchanging information with people

- Employing surveys to collect information about the community's wishes

- Using newsletters, school newspapers, and meetings to get information out to the community

- Inviting parents and community groups into the school

Beacon Elementary School, encountered in Chapter One, provides a good model for inclusive dialogue. Perhaps the most significant practice at Beacon was that those with power—the educators—dropped pretenses to authority. They acted silly, dressed in unique ways, and left testaments to their awards and degrees at home, all in the hope that they would be able to put parents and students at ease. Educators at Beacon took many other measures to include everyone in dialogue, including making themselves available, approaching people in the community, employing newsletters and surveys, and inviting people into the school. The result was that both parents and students felt comfortable enough to interact with the educators and share their thoughts and feelings with them in classrooms, in hallways, on school grounds, and in meetings.

At its best, dialogue encourages the inclusion of voices not normally heard. It would be naïve to think that dialogue in itself, however, can ensure that the marginalized will overturn the entrenched power relationships that exclude them from many of the advantages that others enjoy. Relationships among classed, raced, and gendered students, educators, and parents are difficult to overcome in the classroom and in the school. Even so, we should not dismiss efforts at dialogue out of hand. Even critics see value in it.[55] Although they reject the belief that everyone has equal opportunities to speak and be heard, some critics feel that dialogue can help "build coalitions among multiple, shifting, intersecting and sometimes contradictory groups carrying equal weights of legitimacy."[56] At the very least, dialogue can help people build coalitions with others to support inclusion.

Emphasizing Student Learning and Classroom Practice

While dialogue facilitates critical conversations, it also needs to target student learning. Educating the school community to be critical about issues of inclusion is important. These and other measures will mean little, however, if student learning is not affected. Unfortunately, recent evidence from urban centers in the United States indicates that there is no firm connection between reforms designed to increase inclusion and student achievement.[57] This research shows that changes designed to provide parents with power may not have an impact on achievement if these changes do not specifically target teaching and learning, with the goal of improving both the capacities and the commitment of professional educators. Improving commitment is most easily achieved when educators are aware of practices that work in varied settings and are given the chance to talk critically about their teaching. Educators can support inclusion best in schools in which they establish clear goals, support collaboration, encourage risk taking, and fairly monitor progress.

Research is clear on the best ways of delivering curriculum in inclusive ways. For example, it has found that students are generally included when the school honors different ways of knowing and different sources of knowledge, when it allows students to write and speak in their own vernacular, and when it employs culturally compatible communication styles. Educators can promote inclusion in the classroom when they express cultural solidarity with their students, demonstrate that they care about them, and hold high expectations for all students.[58] There are many ways to put these and other strategies into practice, and teachers and those responsible for supervising teaching ought to talk about them.

Inclusive teaching practice is served when teachers and their supervisors have opportunities to talk about it. Particularly effective are dialogues that encourage teachers to become aware of and critically reflect on their learning and professional practice.[59] The face-to-face communication that is part of this process is based on mutual respect, and it should be reflective and open to critique.[60] But it is not just teachers' talk, action, and beliefs that need to be open to critique; supervisors' talk, action, and beliefs also must be subject to examination. In these interactions, supervisors need to be prepared to give, invite, and receive critiques and to encourage

and instruct others on how to do so as well, thus empowering teachers and making it possible for both parties to work toward inclusion.

How might such critical conversations proceed? Supervisors can
employ six talking strategies:

- Making suggestions

- Giving feedback

- Modeling

- Using inquiry

- Soliciting advice and opinions

- Giving praise[61]

Making suggestions can include the following:

- Listening

- Sharing experiences

- Using examples and demonstrations

- Providing choices for teachers

- Challenging outdated policies

- Encouraging risk taking

- Supplying professional literature

- Recognizing teachers' strengths

- Maintaining a focus on improving instruction[62]

Feedback on teaching should

- Be detailed and specific

- Express caring, interest, and support

- Be nonjudgmental

- Provide praise

- Establish a problem-solving orientation

- Respond to any concerns that teachers, students, or parents might have about student behavior

- Discuss teacher-student interaction[63]

These types of critical conversations occur most often in contexts in which school goals are developed collaboratively and clearly communicated to everyone. This is particularly important in diverse settings because members of various groups may not understand what others in more homogeneous contexts take for granted. It is also important for teachers to be clear about their goals for student achievement, students' ability to meet them, and how students and teachers will know when goals are met. All this occurs most often in schools that make student learning a priority[64]—for example, by hiring teachers who value student achievement, promoting people who hold these values, and endorsing only programs that demonstrate benefits for student learning.[65]

Collaboration can also have a positive impact on teaching and learning in inclusive environments, so leadership efforts should be organized to support it. Schools display support for collaboration when they endorse a philosophy of teamwork, provide time for collaboration, and advocate for sharing and peer observation of instruction. Clearing the way for peers to coach can enhance teaching and learning. Given the right conditions, fellow teachers can devote more time to coaching than administrators can. Teachers, moreover, tend to respect colleagues whom they know possess the experience and expertise to help them. Indeed, classroom training is most effective when peers are involved.[66]

North High School's experience illustrates the effectiveness of this strategy.[67] Its eighty-five staff members teach roughly 1,200 middle-class and lower-middle-class students who come from sub-urban or rural areas. The school's founding principal, David Snow, is now in his sixteenth year. During his tenure, he has successfully developed a system that gives his five division chairs primary responsibility for classroom instruction. The teachers readily accept the efforts of the chairs because they recognize their expertise. Snow has put a number of practices in place to make these arrangements work. He has taken much care in selecting the division chairs, given them the authority to exercise their judgment, provided the preparation time necessary for them to focus on instruction, allowed experimentation, encouraged risk taking, and developed a consensus on school goals and faculty roles. Giving others freedom is not always an easy thing to do, however, as Snow indicates, with respect to one of his division chairs: "I am going to give him some latitude so he can provide the leadership you want from him . . . [and] stay out of [his] way some. Now that can be taken as a lack of interest . . . [which] is probably the most difficult thing for me to do . . . to keep hands off and still communicate that I am interested in what they are doing."[68]

Administrators can provide opportunities for teachers to step into leadership roles, but in many instances, teachers themselves take the initiative to contribute to leadership processes. Yvonne Divans-Hutchison is one such teacher.[69] She teaches English to a diverse student population at King/Drew Magnet School for Medicine and Science in Los Angeles. She has served in many leadership roles, including being part of a literacy cadre, coordinator of other teachers from across disciplines, curriculum coordinator, literacy coach, professional developer, and cochair of the English department. Yvonne was also a member of the second cohort of the Carnegie Academy for the Scholarship of Teaching and Learning Scholars and recently served as a National Board of Professional Teaching Standards scholar and an instructor at the University of California at Los Angeles. Last year, she conducted all of the staff development at her school and was an official mentor for new teachers.

In her leadership activities, Yvonne always assumes her teacher role. This is apparent in the ways that she approaches her different audiences. To compensate for novice teachers' lack of confidence, for instance, Yvonne boosts their view of themselves by getting them to talk about their strengths. In her professional development activities, she uses different techniques with new teachers and with veterans. In this sense, her leadership reflects her beliefs about teaching; Yvonne embraces diversity, shares with and learns from others, models participation, builds habits of mind, engages students in learning, and encourages development of student voices. At the school level, she is supported by a group of colleagues who meet regularly to inspire one another with success stories, exchange ideas, and figure out how to fix trouble spots in their teaching. Both new and veteran teachers meet to celebrate teaching and to affirm the wonders of teaching for each other. Yvonne has also gone public with her work, creating a Web site (http://kml.carnegiefoundation .org/gallery/yhutchinson/index.html) that opens her teaching to a wide audience and reveals just how a teacher thinks, plans, revises, and reflects.

Encouraging and supporting program changes can also contribute to inclusive efforts in the classroom. Teachers need to be able to experiment in relative comfort, particularly with teaching that goes against the grain.[70] They need to have the confidence to try new ideas without fearing the consequences of failure. Thus, schools must nurture an atmosphere that supports experimentation and protects teachers from any fallout that may result. While encouraging community input, they need to shield teachers from unproductive and haphazard intrusions. This requires that school communities channel various community influences into coordinated efforts that help rather than hinder program changes.

School communities also need to ensure that their monitoring of student progress is fair and comprehensive. In doing so, they will have to find the know-how to work within or around existing systems, which, unfortunately, are not all consistent with inclusion.

For example, many recent education reforms have championed evaluation processes that are exclusive. The kind of standardized testing that is currently in vogue can be very harmful to already excluded and marginalized groups.[71] The task for school communities, then, is not so much designing monitoring systems from scratch but tempering or supplementing those that already exist. Consequently, members of the school community must understand the strengths and weaknesses of the various approaches. They need to recognize the harm that certain methods bring with them, attempt to modify the effects, and provide alternate forms of evaluation that are fair to all students. School communities must help teachers use the results of assessment to improve teacher and student learning and to help parents understand where and why improvement is needed.[72] In all of these processes, schools should advocate for groups that are not always well served by current systems of evaluation and by the school system generally.[73]

Adopting Inclusive Policymaking Processes

For schools to be truly inclusive communities, they need to adopt inclusive policymaking processes. Policy deliberations can embrace inclusion in two ways: first, by promoting policies that favor inclusive values and, second, by organizing policy deliberation processes that are themselves inclusive. This means that all interests in the school community are fairly represented in these processes and that they have equal and fair opportunities to influence the outcome of the processes. This is a tall order, particularly in diverse contexts in which efforts to include various communities in school policymaking have not always been successful. Research indicates that some communities prefer not to participate in school activities, let alone ones that involve decision making.[74] Some groups believe that the school—not parents—should be engaged in these activities, while others either do not have the time or lack the confidence to participate. When some groups do come to the table, they often find that they do not have the specialized knowledge required to make their case or that they lack the language they need to enter into conversations.

The first step that schools need to take is to ensure that all community interests are fairly represented among the people engaged in policy deliberations. For this to happen, the circle of policymakers will have to include people who are in touch with the values, interests, and wishes of the people whom the policy affects.[75] Thus, bringing in outsiders—particularly those who don't normally associate themselves with school activities—can improve the policy process. Besides representing various interests, their unique local expertise can broaden interpretations of problem situations and yield fresh insights. Unfortunately, it is not always easy to recruit such individuals to engage in setting policy or making decisions. Schools have to take the initiative to approach individuals and request their help. The best way to ensure that everyone is well represented in such processes is to have favorable school-community relationships in place. This was the case at Richmond Road School in New Zealand (described in Chapter Three); parents there felt comfortable approaching the school at any time and for any reason. They felt just as at ease in deliberating policy matters as they did in offering their expertise in the classroom.[76]

The transition to inclusive practices might prove to be a challenge for some. As I explained in Chapter Three, some participants may be uncertain of or uncomfortable with their new roles; others may be reluctant to accept the power and responsibilities associated with them. Still others may not know how to approach the problems that arise or deal with the inevitable conflict that occurs. To help people ease into these new situations, schools need to use the following strategies:

- Allow local input into the development of their policy-making process

- Design roles that are clearly specified yet not overly constraining

- Nurture a climate that supports risk taking

- Provide support that helps participants solve problems and manage conflicts

- Provide adequate resources—for example, materials to help educate participants; extra help so that teachers can have release time; or materials, people, or in-service sessions to help them manage conflict

- Initiate an ongoing process for educating participants

- Implement new processes gradually

One thing that will help in the initial stages of the policy process is knowing the community—parents, teachers, and students. Schools can acquire this knowledge in a number of ways.[77] For example, they can circulate surveys or make connections with individuals and community agencies. The knowledge that they obtain from using these strategies can boost their understanding of community situations, point to areas that need attention, and sort out the extent to which policies from the government or central office need to be tailored to meet local needs. This information can also help educators respond in appropriate ways to requests from community members—staff, students, parents, or neighbors—for action, often in response to recurring situations.[78]

Once policymakers have been identified, an appropriate environment for the deliberations needs to be established. This includes setting the tone for the meetings. It helps to find a meeting place in which everyone is comfortable; this may require that gatherings be held away from the school. Schools will also have to find ways to give everyone a voice in deliberations. Some researchers believe that administrators need to withdraw from center stage in the process because they may be tempted to use their power to influence the outcome,[79] as research has demonstrated.[80] These researchers go on to suggest that if administrators do participate, they should limit themselves to consultative contributions, offer their opinions last, and make it clear that they will accept any decision arrived at by democratic means. Withdrawing in this manner, however, leaves policymakers to their own devices in settings in which not everyone has equal power. In some situations, this is appropriate; in many others, it is not. In these latter settings, administrators need to use their power to ensure that those with fewer resources can participate in conversations and have fair opportunities to influence the outcome. They can see that the language used is not so specialized or exclusive, so that all can understand and use it; that all members have sufficient background information on the issues under discussion; that everyone has an opportunity to speak their mind; and that no one unfairly dominates deliberations. Administrators may need to work with community members to set rules for meetings that all are comfortable with. Administrators may sometimes need to act as interpreters, clarifying the positions of some members for others and intervening to make sure that deliberations are fair. And administrators must also be mindful that they can never be neutral in their stances and that they might unwittingly dominate deliberations.

The next step in the policy process is identifying the problems associated with the issues at hand.[81] This is not necessarily a straightforward matter, particularly in diverse contexts. People will inevitably see problems in different ways. Some may see persistent conflicts between teachers and students as attempts to take advantage of teachers, while others may view them as indicators of racism. In these cases, efforts should be made to reach consensus on a problem. This means being able to frame it in a language that everyone can agree on. Agreement, however, will not always be forthcoming. If policymakers cannot agree on the language, then the problem should be treated as more than one problem. When there is no consensus, policymakers should be encouraged to adopt other people's problems as their own. They should try to see the world from the different points of view of others. Once the problems have been identified, a range of proposed solutions needs to be discussed and tentatively adopted.

After policymakers complete the first draft of a policy, they need to consult with the people who will be affected by it. Such a process was employed by Mary Seacole Comprehensive, a girls' school of 550 students from the ages of eleven to sixteen, located in a large Midlands city in the United Kingdom.[82] Just under half of the students are of South Asian background, one-third are white, and roughly one-fifth are of African Caribbean background. There are also small numbers of Vietnamese, Greek, and Italian students. The Seacole policymakers made every effort to consult with teachers, students, and the community as they designed a policy to combat racism. They kept teachers informed so that they knew of the development of the policy and its main features. The policy group also sought student involvement. With the support of the school's administration and the student council, the members of the policy group posted a draft of the policy document in every classroom, and all teachers discussed the policy during class. In addition, students were invited to send in written comments. The policy group also tried to consult with members of the community. Students told their parents about the policy and talked to community workers. Drafts of the policy were also sent to community organizations, and individual members of the community were consulted. The policy group received mostly constructive comments on their draft, recruited a few people to help them refine their document, and incorporated many of the suggestions.

Drafting the policy should not be seen as the final step in the process. Policymakers should not be too hasty. New policies need to be tested and monitored and thus should be considered tentative. Policies must go through trial periods during which information is collected on the policy in action. These kinds of trials were conducted at Richmond Road School in New Zealand.[83] Over a number of years, senior teachers and others in the school community conducted trials of a new student grouping structure. Information from teachers and others in the school community played an important part in the adjustments that were eventually made to the policy. Schools should also continue to monitor policies after the initial trial period; changing circumstances may produce new demands and problems. For instance, policies on matters such as course selection and student achievement will always require periodic monitoring and review.[84]

Not all school problems or issues require formal policymaking processes. Setting up policy proceedings for every problem that comes along will take time away from important issues that demand more intense deliberations. Consequently, schools need a mechanism for determining which issues are best addressed by policies and which issues should be handled by particular individuals. Generally speaking, administrators ought to handle the more routine issues. On the other hand, administrators may want to take a middle road on problems that fall somewhere between routine and unique but are not as important as others. They may want to convene a committee or simply consult with those who would be affected by a decision. Whatever path is taken, however, needs to be consistent with an inclusive philosophy.

Incorporating Whole-School Approaches

The point has been made several times that if inclusion is to be successfully promoted in schools, it must become firmly entrenched in day-to-day activities. To increase their prospects for success in these efforts, schools need to involve whole school communities, making inclusion an essential and routine part of educational practice in ways that ensure its longevity and protect it against wider changes in educational policy. Piecemeal or spontaneous responses and initiatives will not be enough. Schools need to nurture school cultures that encourage and support inclusion. This is no easy task, because it requires developing shared sets of values that also include everyone. Unfortunately, not all views of organizational culture are helpful in this regard.

There is no shortage of advice for schools that wish to develop or nurture particular climates or cultures. Much of it comes from a management perspective;[85] its basic premise is that managers will get the most out of their employees if they can find ways to engender in them a motivating or collective ethos or spirit. The idea is that employees—in this case, teachers—will be more committed to the organization if this commitment appears to originate naturally with them rather than being imposed by management. Ironically, much of this literature focuses on the acts that administrators can undertake to induce this sort of commitment. One commonly cited method for administrators is manipulating the symbols with which members of the organization identify. So principals, for example, might use time, resources, and symbolic language to develop shared meanings with staff.[86] Administrators can play other symbol-related roles to foster a shared culture. An administrator might act as (1) a historian who reads current events and reinterprets them for the rest of the staff, (2) an anthropological detective who searches for meaning in the behavior of others, (3) a visionary who projects hope and dreams for the entire staff, or (4) a symbol in himself or herself, making sure that important routines and ceremonies in the school's life are reliable.[87] In the end, though, many of these sorts of strategies represent efforts on the part of administrators to induce members of the school community to buy into a vision that originates not with parents, teachers, or students, but with the administration.

Schools, however, should be cautious about jumping on the culture bandwagon. Critics have pointed out problems with approaching whole-school enterprises in this manner.[88] These difficulties include the ways in which people view culture and the ends to which culture-shaping efforts are directed. Neither is consistent with inclusion. The more bald-faced versions of culture shaping are explicitly manipulative. Supporters of this view mistakenly see culture as a variable, and they encourage administrators to use it to move members of the organization to think and act to promote what they believe to be organizational interests. Unfortunately, these interests do not always coincide with the interests of everyone but are most often those of management, represented in such items as management-generated vision statements. The version of culture that these management gurus employ is also trivial and static.[89] It fails to account for the complexities of culture in organizations like schools, which display more than one culture. Such cultures are dynamic, contested, and rich, and they extend far beyond the boundaries of the schoolhouse.

For schools to promote cultures that foster inclusion, they will need to acknowledge the complexities of culture and be sensitive to the ends to which their efforts are directed. An inclusive approach to leadership demands that the efforts of members of the school community promote everyone's interests, not just those of management or of dominant groups. Vision statements, for example, ought to emanate not only from management or from powerful individuals and groups but equitably from all segments of the school community. Whatever shared values emerge from whole-school efforts to incorporate inclusion must represent all groups, and all groups must benefit equitably from these values. Schools need to find ways to make space for traditionally excluded cultures to be part of the process of building a shared vision and shared values. Their values and lifestyles should be honored and thus incorporated into the content and process of schooling.

For schools to enshrine whole-school practices that are consistent with inclusion, they will have to ensure that more than a few members of the school community understand the practices in similar ways. In other words, schools need to work at building meanings that favor the values of inclusion. No educational enterprise will succeed if students, teachers, parents, and administrators do not share some common understandings about inclusive values. This is not to say that it will always be possible for everyone to come to similar understandings in contemporary diverse school contexts; but there will need to be at least some level of agreement—however fleeting and fluid—in order for cultural dynamics to work out for the best. Meanings can be shaped through day-to-day management of meaning (for example, when administrators interpret policy for teachers), through mediation of conflict, and through resolution of contradictions in positions.[90] Prominent individuals, such as administrators, need to be careful not to unilaterally impose their own meanings on others, however, as would proponents of the corporate culture view. Rather, they need to engage everyone in critical conversations. These conversations represent the best option for negotiating fairly the construction of meanings that work in the interests of all groups. Because these meanings will never be permanent, however, everyone has to continually work at this process.

Mary Seacole Comprehensive worked to entrench inclusive practices—in particular, practices to combat racism—in its school culture.[91] Efforts to routinize practices to combat racism received initial impetus from the head teacher, who signaled her support by settling a long-running dispute about Muslim young women and uniform requirements. She provided a space for a core group of teachers to begin to promote their beliefs about and practices for combating racism by conferring status on their work and providing resources. With this support, the group began to take their views to a wider audience in the school, organizing in-service events, making explicit statements about school policy, and challenging colleagues. In time, their tactics shifted from taking aggressive and essentialist positions to having a more reflective and enabling dialogue. The group sponsored professional development activities that looked outside the school to engage communities and inside the school to examine classroom practices. Outside speakers were brought in to break down people's ignorance and suspicion of local communities, and staff were encouraged to apply new perspectives to their specific experiences and concerns as classroom teachers. Sessions instructed teachers in how they might use curriculum materials to address issues of racism and to challenge common stereotypes. Eventually, this perspective against racism spread and took hold. Now an established part of life at Seacole, it continues to be extended as new teachers are carefully chosen and inducted into the school culture.

Ensuring Meaningful Inclusion

The basic premise of this book is that schools and communities will be better places when everyone is included. Such an ideal is not new; many individuals and groups have embraced it over the years. One of the better-known expressions of this idea is in the U.S. Constitution. Penned in the eighteenth century, one of the most familiar passages reads, "We hold these truths to be self-evident, that all men are created equal, that they are endowed by their Creator with certain unalienable rights, that among these are life, liberty and the pursuit of happiness."

These principles provided the foundation for a nation and, indeed, in time, with some variations, for many nations. Because they perceived injustice in the American colonies, the framers sought to embed equality in the constitution of a country. They hoped that their new country would be a place where everyone would be able to participate freely in their community; no one would be unnecessarily excluded, as many had been before 1776.

The U.S. Constitution represents a landmark achievement. However, for those looking for equality in the present day, it is also an ironic document. To begin with, the very language it employs is exclusive. The use of the term *men* is exclusive, whether it was meant to stand for women and men (and children, too) or just men. It is difficult to blame the founding fathers for such an oversight. They lived in a time when only men were involved in political matters and women were all but invisible. The exclusive language would probably not have been something they would have recognized, because the subservient position of women would have been taken for granted. It is also ironic that this document was fashioned while slavery was still an accepted practice. In fact, the task of some participants in the constitutional talks was to see that the new constitution did not infringe on the right to enslave people. The bottom line is that the perspective from which the architects of the U.S. Constitution approached their task blinded them to certain kinds of inequality. This same reality also makes it difficult for contemporary educators to follow through on the honorable intentions of the Constitution. Many well-intentioned people do not always recognize the extent or variable nature of inequality and exclusion and thus have difficulty putting their inclusive ideals into practice.

The attainment of inclusion in schools and wider communities requires both that leadership practices be organized to achieve it and that leadership practices be inclusive. Leadership should be seen as a collective process, not as something to be identified exclusively with particular individuals. School communities also need to work at developing and sustaining learning activities that can expose the depth and breadth of often taken-for-granted but debilitating exclusive practices so that such practices can be eliminated. Although the task is challenging, schools can achieve inclusive ideals; we have seen many instances in this book. Schools have enabled a wide range of groups to become meaningfully involved in what schools have to offer, often as a result of relatively small groups of students, teachers, parents, and administrators' displaying courage, compassion, and commitment to inclusion by banding together to promote inclusion in their schools and communities. We can take hope from anthropologist Margaret Mead's statement: "Never doubt that a small group of thoughtful, committed citizens can change the world. Indeed, it's the only thing that ever has."

It is now up to the rest of us to take heed of these accomplishments and do what we can to promote inclusion in our own institutions and communities. Failing to do this is not an option, for the future of our schools and our world depends on it.

Notes

Chapter One

1. The names of the school, the principal, and the vice principal are pseudonyms.

2. Personal communication, March 2004.

3. S. May (1994), *Making multicultural education work* (Clevedon, U.K.: Multilingual Matters); C. Giles & A. Hargreaves (in press), The sustainability of innovative schools as learning organizations and professional learning communities during standardized reform, *Educational Administration Quarterly*.

4. Educational Testing Service State and Federal Relations Office (2002), *The No Child Left Behind Act: A special report* (Revised) (Washington, DC: Author). Despite the title of this legislation, it is, in many respects, exclusive.

5. Educational Testing Service State and Federal Relations Office (2002).

6. L. McNeil (2000), *Contradictions of school reform: Educational costs of standard testing* (New York: Routledge).

7. This management-oriented view is not unique; it has often accompanied recent restructuring efforts in other industries as well as in education. See J. Blackmore (1999), *Troubling women: Feminism, leadership and educational change* (Buckingham, U.K.: Open University Press); S. Gewirtz (2002), *The managerial school: Post-welfarism and social justice in education* (New York: Routledge); S. Gewirtz &

S. Ball (2000), From "welfarism" to "new managerialism": Shifting discourses of school leadership in the education marketplace, *Discourse: Studies in the Cultural Politics of Education, 21*(3), 253–268.

8. Giles & Hargreaves (in press).

9. Giles & Hargreaves (in press).

10. G. Anderson (1998), Toward authentic participation: Deconstructing the discourses of participatory reforms in education, *American Educational Research Journal, 35*(4), 571–603.

11. Anderson (1998); M. Fine (1993), [Ap]parent involvement: Reflections on parents, power, and urban public schools, *Teachers College Record, 94*(4), 682–710; R. Hatcher, B. Troyna, & D. Gewirtz (1996), *Racial equality and the local management of schools* (Stattfordshire, U.K.: Trentham Books); B. Malen & R. Ogawa (1992), Community involvement: Parents, teachers and administrators working together, in S. Bacharach (Ed.), *Education reform: Making sense of it all* (Toronto: Allyn & Bacon), 103–119.

12. J. Ryan (2002), Educational leadership in contexts of diversity and accountability: A review, in K. Leithwood & P. Hallinger (Eds.), *The second international handbook of educational leadership and administration* (Dordrecht, Netherlands: Kluwer), 979–1002.

13. M. Loeb (1994, September), Where leaders come from, *Fortune*, 41–42; Ryan (2002).

14. P. Hallinger & R. Heck (1998), Exploring the principal's contribution to school effectiveness: 1980–1995, *School Effectiveness and School Improvement, 9*(2), 157–191.

15. P. Gronn (2002), Distributed leadership, in K. Leithwood & P. Hallinger (Eds.), *The second international handbook of educational leadership and administration* (Dordrecht, Netherlands: Kluwer), 653–696; D. Pounder, R. Ogawa, & E. Adams (1995), Leadership as an organization-wide phenomenon: Its impact on school performance, *Educational Administration Quarterly, 31*(4), 564–588; J. Spillane, R. Halverson, & J. Diamond (2001), Investigating school leadership practice: A distributed perspective, *Educational Researcher, 30*(3), 23–28.

16. M. Smylie, S. Conley, & H. Marks (2002), Building leadership into the roles of teachers, in J. Murphy (Ed.), *The educational leadership challenge: Redefining leadership for the 21st century* (Chicago: National Society for the Study of Education), 162–188. I realize that pragmatic reasons can be moral ones and that moral reasons can also be pragmatic. By *pragmatic*, I mean being included to generate a particular end. So the argument for teacher inclusion might be that it would improve morale or student achievement. In using the word *moral*, I am referring to the right to be included regardless of the outcome. The argument is that teachers should be included in decision making because they have that right, not necessarily because it may improve morale or student achievement.

17. The jury is still out on the relationship between teacher leadership and student achievement and school improvement. See M. Smylie (1997), Research on teacher leadership: Assessing the state of the art, in B. Biddle, T. Good, & I. Goodson (Eds.), *International handbook of teachers and teaching* (Dordrecht, Netherlands: Kluwer), 521–592.

18. See, for example, D. Byrne (1999), *Social exclusion* (Philadelphia: Open University Press); G. Dei, S. James-Wilson, & J. Zine (2002), *Inclusive schooling: A teacher's guide to removing the margins* (Toronto: Canadian Scholar's Press); K. Riley & E. Rustique-Forrester (2002), *Working with disaffected students* (London: Paul Chapman).

19. *Webster's new world dictionary of the American language* (New York: World, 1960).

20. A. Walker & C. Walker (Eds.) (1997), *Britain divided: The growth of social exclusion in the 1980s and 1990s* (London: Child Poverty Action Group); A. Madanipour, G. Cars, & J. Allen (Eds.) (1998), *Social exclusion in European cities* (London: Jessica Kingsley).

21. See, for example, J. Bailey & D. du Plessis (1997), Understanding principals' attitudes toward inclusive schooling, *Journal of Educational Administration, 35*(5), 428–438; R. Thomas with S. Macanawai & C. MacLaurin (1997), Editorial, *Journal of Educational Administration, 35*(5), 385–396.

22. M. Keys, C. Hanley-Maxwell, & C. Capper (1999), Spirituality? It's the core of my leadership: Empowering leadership in an inclusive elementary school, *Educational Administration Quarterly, 35*(2), 203.

23. Dei, James-Wilson, & Zine (2002).

24. Dei, James-Wilson, & Zine (2002).

25. M. Richmon & D. Allison (2003), Toward a conceptual framework for leadership inquiry, *Educational Management and Administration, 13*(1), 31–50.

26. G. Yukl (1994), *Leadership in organizations* (Englewood Cliffs, NJ: Prentice Hall).

27. Influence or power need not be seen only in terms of people; it can also take the form of social forces or phenomena that transcend individual men and women. Sociologists like Emile Durkheim and philosophers like Michel Foucault champion the latter view.

28. D. Corson (2000), Emancipatory leadership, *International Journal of Leadership in Education, 3*(2), 93–120.

Chapter Two

1. *Webster's New World Dictionary of the American Language* (New York: World, 1960).

2. This is a pseudonym.

3. J. Ryan (1988), Economic development and Innu settlement: The establishment of Sheshatshi, *Canadian Journal of Native Studies, 8*(1), 1–25.

4. J. Ryan (1998), Towards a new age in Innu education: Innu resistance and community activism, *Language, Culture and Curriculum, 11*(3), 339–353.

5. J. Ryan (1992), Aboriginal learning styles: A critical review, *Language, Culture and Curriculum, 5*(3), 161–183.

6. J. Ryan (1989), Disciplining the Innut: Normalization, characterization and schooling, *Curriculum Inquiry, 19*(4), 379–403.

7. J. Ryan (1988), *Disciplining the Innut: Social form and control in community, bush and school,* unpublished doctoral dissertation, University of Toronto.

8. Ryan (1998).

9. National Center for Education Statistics (2003), *Statistics and trends in the education of Hispanics: Grade retention, suspension and expulsion* (http://nces.ed.gov/pubs2003/hispanics/Section2.asp).

10. K. E. Riley & E. Rustique-Forrester (2002), *Working with disaffected students* (London: Paul Chapman).

11. A. Osler & J. Hill (1998), Exclusion from school and racial equality: An examination of government proposals in light of recent research evidence, *Cambridge Journal of Education, 28*(1), 33–59.

12. National Center for Education Statistics (2003).

13. P. Bourdieu (1991), *Language and symbolic power* (G. Raymond & M. Adamson, Trans.; introduced by J. B. Thompson, Ed.) (Cambridge, MA: Harvard University Press).

14. Bourdieu (1991).

15. See, for example, D. Sadker & M. Sadker, *Failing at fairness: How America's schools cheat girls* (Toronto: Maxwell MacMillan, 1994).

16. See, for example, J. Shapiro, T. Sewell, & J. Ducette (2001), *Reframing diversity in education* (London: Scarecrow).

17. Hargreaves emphasizes how dignity and respect are eroded in these kinds of situations. See A. Hargreaves (2004), Distinction and disgust: The emotional politics of school failure, *International Journal of Leadership in Education, 7*(4), 27–42.

18. G. Dei, S. James-Wilson, & J. Zine (2002), *Inclusive schooling: A teacher's guide to removing the margins* (Toronto: Canadian Scholar's Press).

19. See, for example, Ontario's Education Act of 1990.

20. M. Falvey, C. Givner, & C. Kimm (1994), What is an inclusive school? in R. Villa & J. Thousand (Eds.), *Creating an inclusive*

school (Alexandria, VA: Association for Supervision and Curriculum Development), 1–12.

21. B. Levin & J. Riffel (2000), Changing schools in a changing world, in N. Bascia & A. Hargreaves (Eds.), *The sharp edge of educational change: Teaching, leading and the realities of reform* (London: Falmer Press), 178–194.

22. J. Coleman, E. Campbell, C. Hobson, A. Mood, F. Winfield, & R. York (1966), *Equality of educational opportunity* (Washington, DC: Government Printing Office); B. Goldstein (1967), *Low income youth in urban areas: A critical review of the literature* (New York: Holt, Rinehart & Winston); C. Jencks (1972), *Inequality: A reassessment of the effect of family and schooling in America* (New York: Basic Books); G. Natriello, E. McDill, & A. Pallas (1990), *Schooling disadvantaged children: Racing against catastrophe* (New York: Teachers College Press).

23. W. Sewell & R. Hauser (1976), Causes and consequences of higher education: Modes of the attainment process, in W. Sewell, R. Hauser, & D. Featherman (Eds.), *Schooling and achievement in American society* (New York: Academic Press), 9–28.

24. J. Karabel (1972), Community colleges and social stratification: Submerged class conflict in American higher education, *Harvard Educational Review, 42,* 521–562.

25. D. Byrne (1999), *Social exclusion* (Philadelphia: Open University Press).

26. W. Hutton (2002), *The world we're in* (London: Little, Brown).

27. Byrne (1999), 82.

28. U.S. Census Bureau (2003), *Historical income tables: Income equality* (www.census.gov/hhes/income/histinc/le3.html).

29. U.S. Census Bureau (2004), *Income stable, poverty up, numbers of Americans with and without health insurance rise, Census Bureau Reports* (http://www.census.gov/Press-Release/www/releases/archives/income_wealth/002484.html).

30. L. Keister (2000), *Wealth in America: Trends in wealth inequality* (Cambridge, U.K.: Cambridge University Press).

31. Byrne (1999).

32. Rich getting richer, middle class poorer: Stats Canada (2002, March 15), *Toronto Star*.

33. Byrne (1999), 81.

34. Byrne (1999).

35. J. Morenoff & M. Tienda (1997), Underclass neighborhoods in temporal and ecological perspective, *Annuals of the American Academy of Political and Social Science, 551*, 59–72.

36. New Jersey State Department of Education (1994), *Comprehensive compliance investigation of the Newark public schools* (Trenton: New Jersey State Department of Education), 43–44, cited in J. Anyon (1997), *Ghetto schooling: A political economy of urban educational reform* (New York: Teachers College Press).

37. J. Anyon (1980), Social class and the hidden curriculum of work, *Journal of Education, 162*, 67–92; J. Anyon (1981), Social class and school knowledge, *Curriculum Inquiry, 11*, 3–42.

38. Anyon (1981), 12.

39. Anyon (1997).

40. G. Whitty, S. Power, & D. Halpin (1998), *Devolution and choice in education: The school, the state and the market* (Melbourne: Australian Council for Educational Research).

41. Whitty, Power, & Halpin (1998).

42. M. Baker & M. Foote (in press), Changing spaces: Urban school interrelationships and the impact of standards-based reform, *Educational Administration Quarterly*.

43. C. Persell (1993), Social class and educational equality, in J. Banks & C. McGee Banks (Eds.), *Multicultural education: Issues and perspectives* (2nd ed.). (Boston: Allyn & Bacon), 71–89.

44. J. Ryan (1999), *Race and ethnicity in multiethnic schools* (Clevedon, U.K.: Multilingual Matters).

45. Even so, only 4,017,000 of the 19,766,000 who immigrated to the United States between 1980 and 1990 emigrated from Europe. See,

for example, U.S. Bureau of the Census (1995), *Statistical abstract of the United States: 1995* (115th ed.). (Washington, DC: Author).

46. U.S. Census Bureau (2001), *Projections of the resident population by age, sex, race and Hispanic origin: 1999 to 2000* (http://www.census .gov/) (Accessed December 11, 2001).

47. B. Merchant (2000), Education and changing demographics, in B. A. Jones (Ed.), *Educational leadership: Policy dimensions in the 21st century* (Stanford, CT: Ablex), 83–90; National Center for Education Statistics (2003), *Racial ethnic distribution of public school students* (http://nces.ed.gov/programs/coe/2002/section1/indicator03 .asp).

48. National Center for Education Statistics (2003).

49. C. Bennett (2001), Genres of research in multicultural education, *Review of Educational Research, 71*(2), 171–217; L. Darling-Hammond (1995), Inequality and access to knowledge, in J. Banks & C. McGee Banks (Eds.), *Handbook of research on multicultural education* (Toronto: Macmillan), 465–483; J. Ogbu (1994), Racial stratification and education in the United States: Why inequality persists, *Teachers College Record, 96,* 264–271; J. Paquette (1990), Minority participation in secondary education: A fine-grained descriptive methodology, *Educational Evaluation and Policy Analysis 13*(2), 139–158.

50. Bennett (2001); College Board (1985), *Equality and excellence: The educational status of Black Americans* (New York: Author); J. Oakes (1985), *Keeping track: How schools structure inequality* (New Haven, CT: Yale University Press); G. Orfield (1999), Politics matters: Educational policy and Chicano students, in J. Moreno (Ed.), *The elusive quest for equality* [Special issue]. *Harvard Educational Review,* 111–119.

51. Bennett (2001); G. Orfield (1988), Exclusion of the majority: Shrinking public access and public policy in metropolitan Los Angeles, *Urban Review, 20*(3), 147–163; Orfield (1999).

52. While Asian students may often exceed other groups of students, many also struggle in schools. See S. Lee (1996), *Unraveling the*

"model minority" stereotype (New York: Teachers College Press); J. Macias (1993), Forgotten history: Educational and social antecedents of high achievement among Asian immigrants in the United States, *Curriculum Inquiry 23*(4), 409–423; Paquette (1990); Ryan (1999).

53. J. Lee (2002), Racial and ethnic achievement gap trends: Reversing the progress towards equity? *Educational Researcher, 31*(1), 3–12.

54. Ryan (1999).

55. G. Dei, J. Mazzuca, E. McIsaac, & J. Zine (1997), *Reconstructing "drop-out": A critical ethnography of the dynamics of black students' disengagement from school* (Toronto: University of Toronto Press), 139.

56. Ryan (1999).

57. Ryan (1999), 106.

58. Ryan (1999), 105.

59. S. Lawrence-Lightfoot (1978), *Worlds apart: Relationships between schools and families* (New York: Basic Books).

60. J. Ogbu (1987), Variability in minority school performance: A problem in search of an explanation, *Anthropology and Education Quarterly, 18*(4), 312–334.

61. Singled out (2002, October 19), *Toronto Star* (http://www.thestar.com/NASApp/cs/ContentServer?pagename=thestar/Render&c=Page&cid=968332188492) (Accessed October 19, 2002).

62. S. Contenta (2002, November 8), U.K. to target police racism, *Toronto Star* (http://www.thestar.com/NASApp/cs/ContentServer?pagename=thestar/Render&c=Page&cid=968332188492) (Accessed November 8, 2002); S. Contenta (2003, October 23), Racism exposé rocks U.K. police, *Toronto Star* (http://www.thestar.com/NASApp/cs/ContentServer?pagename=thestar/Render&c=Page&cid=968332188492) (Accessed October 23, 2003); S. Wortley (in press), The usual suspects: Race, police stops and perceptions of criminal injustice, *Criminology* (This paper was also presented at the 48th annual conference of the American

Society of Criminology, November 1997.); C. E. James (1998), "Up to no good": Black on the streets and encountering police, in V. Satzewich (Ed.), *Racism and social inequality in Canada: Concepts, controversies and strategies of resistance* (Toronto: Thompson Educational Publishing), 157–172; Ontario Human Rights Commission (2003), *Paying the price: The human cost of racial profiling inquiry* (http://www.ohrc.on.ca/english/ consultations/racial-profiling-report.shtml).

63. A. Schlesinger (1991), *The disuniting of America* (Knoxville, TN: Whittle Direct), 58. For a Canadian version of this opinion, see N. Bissoondath (1994), *Selling illusions: The cult of multiculturalism in Canada* (Toronto: Penguin).

64. D. Morely & K. Robbins (1995), *Spaces of identity: Global, electronic landscapes and cultural boundaries* (London: Routledge), 89.

65. P. Buchanan (2002), *The death of the West: How dying populations and immigrant invasions imperil our country and civilization* (New York: St. Martin's Press), 2.

66. H. Giroux (2002), Democracy, freedom and justice after September 11th: Rethinking the role of educators and the politics of schooling, *Teachers College Record* (http://www.tcrecord.org/ Content.asp?ContentID=10871) (Accessed November 10, 2003).

67. M. Davis (2001), The flames of New York, *New Left Review, 12*, 34–50.

68. Giroux (2002).

69. C. Szustaczek (2002), U.S border law keeps prof home, *The CAUT Bulletin* [Canadian Association of University Teachers], 8, 3.

70. Szustaczek (2002), 3.

71. J. Blackmore (1999), *Troubling women: Feminism, leadership and educational change* (Philadelphia: Open University Press); B. Young (2002), The Alberta advantage: "DeKleining" career prospects for women educators, in C. Reynolds (Ed.), *Women and school leadership* (Albany: State University of New York Press), 75–92.

72. H. Wagemaker (Ed.) (1996), *Are girls better readers? Gender differences in reading literacy in 32 countries* (Amsterdam: International

Association for the Evaluation of Educational Achievement); Education Quality and Accountability Office (2002), *Ontario secondary school literacy test: Report of provincial results* (Toronto: Queen's Printer for Ontario).

73. Young (2002).

74. B. Young & S. Ansara (1999), Women in educational administration: Statistics for a decade, *ATA Magazine, 79*(2), 22–27.

75. Shapiro, Sewell, & Ducette (2001).

76. One of these decisions was made in Ontario.

77. A. Kodias & J. Jones (1991), A contextual examination of the feminization of poverty, *Geoforum, 22*(2), 159–171.

78. J. Rodgers, The relationship between poverty and household type, in D. Papadimitiou (Ed.), *Aspects of distribution of wealth and income* (London: Macmillan, 1994).

79. Byrne (1999).

80. Kodias & Jones (1991).

81. D. Harvey (1989), *The condition of postmodernity* (Oxford, U.K.: Blackwell), 153.

82. Young (2002).

83. Young (2002).

84. M. Grogan (1996), *Voices of women aspiring to the superintendency* (Albany: State University of New York Press); R. Rees (1990), *Women and men in education* (Ottawa: Canadian Education Association); M. Tallerico (1999), Women and the superintendency: What do we really know? in C. Brunner (Ed.), *Sacred dreams: Women and the superintendency* (Albany: State University of New York Press), 29–48.

85. Young & Ansara (1999).

86. Statistics Canada (1998). *Education in Canada, 1997.* (Ottawa: Ministry of Supply and Services).

87. Canadian Teachers Federation (1999, December–January), Female educators still underrepresented in school administration, *Economic Service Notes* (Ottawa: Author).

88. National Center for Education Statistics (2002), *Elementary and secondary education* (http://nces.ed.gov/programs/digest/d02/tables/dt085.asp).

89. Young (2002); Blackmore (1999).

90. P. Orenstein (2002), Striking back: Sexual harassment at Weston, in *The Jossey-Bass reader on gender in education* (San Francisco: Jossey-Bass), 459–475.

91. N. Stein (2002), Bullying as sexual harassment in elementary schools, in *The Jossey-Bass reader on gender in education* (San Francisco: Jossey-Bass) 409–428.

92. A. Datnow (1998), *The gender politics of educational change* (London: Falmer Press).

93. C. Lugg (2003), Sissies, faggots, lezzies and dykes: Gender, sexual orientation, and a new politics of education? *Educational Administration Quarterly, 39*(1), 95–134.

94. D. Knapp (1999, October 6), 1 year after Shepard killing, tougher hate crimes laws still sought (http://www.cnn.com/US/9910/06/shepard.anniversary/). See also Lugg (2003).

95. Young, gay and scared to death at school (1999, September 23) (http://www.cnn.com/US/9909/23/hate.crimes.gays/).

96. W. McFarland (2001), The legal duty to protect gay and lesbian students from violence in school, *Professional School Counseling, 4*(3), 171–180.

97. M. Tabor (1992, June 14), For gay high-school senior, nightmare is almost over, *New York Times*.

98. Shapiro, Sewell, & Ducette (2001).

99. J. Sears (1993), Responding to the sexual diversity of faculty and students: Sexual praxis and the critical reflective administrator, in C. Capper (Ed.), *Educational administration in a pluralistic society* (Albany: State University of New York Press), 110–172.

100. J. Blount (2003), Homosexuality and school superintendents: A brief history, *Journal of School Leadership, 13*, 7–26.

101. Blount (2003).

102. D. Fraynd & C. Capper (2003), "Do you have any idea who you just hired?!?" A study of open and closeted sexual minority K–12 administrators, *Journal of School Leadership, 13,* 108.

103. Fraynd & Capper (2003), 104.

104. U.S. Census Bureau (2003), Poverty, income see slight changes; child poverty rate unchanged, Census Bureau reports (http:// www.census.gov/Press-Release/www/2003/cb03–153.html). I used the category associated with definition 14 plus net imputed return on equity on own home.

105. Black males are overrepresented among school dropouts and in disciplinary referrals, absenteeism, suspensions and expulsions, programs for the emotionally disturbed, and special education. They also test below average in nearly every academic area. See G. Cartledge, L. Tillman, & C. Johnson (2001), Professional ethics within the context of student discipline and diversity, *Teacher Education and Special Education, 24*(1), 23–37; L. Davis (Ed.) (1999), *Working with African American males: A guide to practice* (London: Sage); B. Harry & M. Anderson (1994), The disproportionate placement of African American males in special education programs: A critical analysis of the process, *Journal of Negro Education, 63*(4), 602–619; R. Hopkins (1997), *Educating black males: Critical lessons in schooling, community, and power* (Albany: State University of New York Press); G. Ladson-Billings (1995), But that's just good teaching! The case for culturally relevant pedagogy, *Theory into Practice, 34*(1), 159–165; J. Nuby & L. Doebler (2000), Issues affecting the recruitment and retention of black students in teacher education, *Negro Educational Review, 51*(3–4), 125–137; V. Polite & J. Davis (Eds.) (1999), *African American males in school and society: Practices and policies for effective education* (New York: Teachers College Press); R. Skiba & R. Peterson (1999), The dark side of zero tolerance: Can punishment lead to safe schools? *Phi Delta Kappan, 80*(5), 372–376, 381–382.

106. See, for example, C. LeDuff (2004, October 13), Mexican-Americans struggle for jobs, *New York Times*.

107. See, for example, F. Fiedler (1967), *A theory of leadership effectiveness* (New York: McGraw-Hill); H. Simon (1947), *Administrative behavior* (New York: Free Press).

108. For a critique, see T. Greenfield & P. Ribbins (1993), *Greenfield on educational administration: Towards a humane science* (London: Routledge).

109. S. Gewirtz (2002), *The managerial school: Post-welfarism and social justice in education* (New York: Routledge).

110. The term *humanist* or *humanistic* is perhaps more familiar to sociologists and philosophers than it is to management researchers or educational administration scholars. The latter may associate the term with a human relations approach to administration—the idea that administrators need to attend to the human side of the people who work in organizations. This is not what I intend to convey with this particular category. Rather, I want to convey the idea that this approach to leadership assumes that it is individuals—as opposed to social phenomena such as discourses—that are responsible for shaping organizations. Moreover, *humanist* is a general term that may subsume other, more specific labels such as *subjectivist* or *phenomenologist*.

111. See, for example, M. Fullan (2003), *The moral imperative of school leadership* (Toronto: Ontario Principals' Council); T. Sergiovanni (1992), *Moral leadership: Getting to the heart of school reform* (San Francisco: Jossey-Bass).

112. B. Bass & B. Aviolo (1993), Transformational leadership: A response to critics, in M. Chemers & R. Ayman (Eds.), *Leadership theory and research: Perspectives and directions* (San Diego, CA: Academic Press), 49–80; B. Bass & B. Aviolo (1993), *Improving organizational effectiveness through transformational leadership* (Thousand Oaks, CA: Sage).

113. J. Burns (1978), *Leadership* (New York: Harper & Row), 20.

114. K. Leithwood & D. Duke (1996), A century's quest to understand school leadership, in K. Leithwood, J. Chapman, D. Corson, P. Hallinger, & A. Hart (Eds.), *International handbook of educational leadership and administration* (Dordrecht, Netherlands: Kluwer), 45–72.

115. It is interesting that the scholar who first used the term *transformational*, Burns, later developed a position that favored social justice; see Burns (1978).

116. P. Gronn (1995), Greatness re-visited: The current obsession with transformational leadership, *Leading and Managing, 1*(1), 14–27.

117. Gronn (1995). There are exceptions, however. See B. Aviolo & B. Bass (1998), Transformational leadership, charisma and beyond, in J. Hunt, B. Baliga, H. Dachler, & C. Schriesheim (Eds.), *Emerging leadership vistas* (Lexington, MA: Lexington Books), 29–49.

118. V. Vanderslice (1988), Separating leadership from leaders: An assessment of the effectiveness of leader and follower roles, *Human Relations, 41*(9), 677–696; P. Gronn (1999), Leadership from a distance: Institutionalizing values and forming character at Timbertop, 1951–61, in P. Begley & P. Leonard (Eds.), *The values of educational administration* (London: Falmer Press), 140–167.

119. K. Leithwood, D. Jantzi, & R. Steinbach (1999a), Changing leadership: A menu of possibilities, in *Changing leadership for changing times* (Buckingham, U.K.: Open University Press); M. Smylie, S. Conley, & H. Marks (2002), Building leadership into the roles of teachers, in J. Murphy (Ed.), *The educational leadership challenge: Redefining leadership for the 21st century* (Chicago: National Society for the Study of Education), 162–188.

Chapter Three

1. I do not use site-based management as a distinct category here because it falls into too many of the other designations. I do, however, use studies and reviews that go by this name to supplement literature in a number of the leadership genres that I employ. For a

thorough review of this body of literature, see B. Malen, R. Ogawa, & J. Kranz (1990), What do we know about school-based management? A case study of the literature—A call for research, in W. Clune & J. Witte (Eds.), *Choice and control in American education: Vol. 2. The practice of choice, decentralization and school restructuring* (New York: Falmer Press), 289–242.

2. B. Fay (1987), *Critical social science* (Ithaca, NY: Cornell University Press).

3. J. Ryan (1998), Critical leadership for education in a postmodern world: Emancipation, resistance and communal action, *International Journal of Leadership in Education, 3*(1), 257–278.

4. A. Giddens (1981), *A contemporary critique of historical materialism* (Berkeley: University of California Press).

5. See V. Robinson (1994), The practical promise of critical research in educational administration, *Educational Administration Quarterly, 30*(1), 56–76.

6. D. Corson (1996a), Emancipatory discursive practices, in K. Leithwood, J. Chapman, D. Corson, P. Hallinger, & A. Hart (Eds.), *International handbook of educational leadership and administration* (Dordrecht, Netherlands: Kluwer), 1043–1067.

7. J. Blackmore (1989), Educational leadership: A feminist critique and reconstruction, in J. Smyth (Ed.), *Critical perspectives on educational leadership* (London: Falmer Press, 1989); G. Grace (1995), *School leadership: Beyond education management* (London: Falmer Press).

8. J. Blackmore (1999), *Troubling women* (Buckingham, U.K., Open University Press); K. Ferguson (1984), *The feminist case against bureaucracy* (Philadelphia: Temple University Press); S. Grundy (1993), Educational leadership as emancipatory praxis, in J. Blackmore and J. Kenway (Eds.), *Gender matters in educational administration and policy* (London, Falmer Press); J. Ogza, *Women in educational management* (Philadelphia: Open University Press, 1993).

9. W. Tierney (1989), Advancing democracy: A critical interpretation of leadership, *Peabody Journal of Education, 66*(3), 157–175; W. Foster, Towards a critical practice of leadership (1989), in

J. Smyth (Ed.), *Critical perspectives on educational Leadership* (London: Falmer Press).

10. E. Rusc (1998), Leadership in evolving democratic school communities, *Journal of School Leadership*, 8, 214–250.

11. D. Corson, Emancipatory leadership (2000), *International Journal of Leadership in Education*, 3(2), 93–120; Corson (1996a); W. Foster (1994), School leaders as transformative intellectuals: Toward a critical pragmaticism, *Advances in Educational Administration*, 3, 29–51; J. Smyth (1996), The socially just alternative to the "self-managing school," in K. Leithwood, J. Chapman, D. Corson, P. Hallinger, & A. Hart (Eds.), *International handbook of educational leadership and administration* (Dordrecht, Netherlands: Kluwer), 1097–1131; J. Ryan (2000), Inclusive leadership for ethnically diverse schools: Initiating and sustaining dialogue, in H. Fennell (Ed.), *The role of the principal in Canada* (Calgary, Canada: Detselig), 119–141; J. Ryan (2003a), *Leading diverse schools* (Dordrecht, Netherlands: Kluwer).

12. N. Burbules (1993), *Dialogue in teaching: Theory and practice* (New York: Teachers College Press).

13. Ryan (2002), Educational leadership in contexts of diversity and accountability: A review, in K. Leithwood & P. Hallinger (Eds.), *The second international handbook of educational leadership and administration* (Dordrecht, Netherlands: Kluwer), 979–1002; Ryan (2003a).

14. Grundy (1993).

15. G. Anderson (1990), Toward a critical constructivist approach to school administration: Invisibility, legitimation and the study of non-events, *Educational Administration Quarterly*, 26(1), 38–59; J. Blase & G. Anderson (1995), *The micropolitics of educational leadership: From control to empowerment* (New York: Teachers College Press).

16. Schools in Ontario are now audited regularly, but there is nothing educational about this audit. It is concerned first and foremost with seeing that schools correctly record the attendance of students.

17. Smyth (1996), 1111.

18. F. Rizvi, Race, gender and the cultural assumptions of schooling, in C. Marshall (Ed.), *The new politics of race and gender* (Bristol, PA: Falmer Press, 1993), 203–217; Ryan (2003a); A. Walker & J. Walker (1998), Challenging the boundaries of sameness: Leadership through valuing difference, *Journal of Educational Administration*, 36(1), 8–28.

19. Ryan (2003a).

20. Blase & Anderson (1995).

21. Blase & Anderson (1995).

22. U. Reitzug (1994), A case study of empowering principal behavior, *American Educational Research Journal* 31(2), 283–307.

23. Reitzug (1994), 295.

24. Reitzug (1994), 299.

25. Reitzug (1994), 302.

26. S. May (1994), *Making multicultural education work* (Clevedon, U.K.: Multilingual Matters).

27. May (1994), 80.

28. May (1994), 71.

29. May (1994), 82–83.

30. May (1994), 66.

31. S. May, On what might have been: Some reflections on critical multiculturalism, in G. Shacklock & J. Smyth (Eds.), *Being reflexive in critical educational and social research* (London: Falmer Press, 1998), 150–170. Recently, Richmond Road appears to have had a rebirth of sorts. Among other things, it has retained some of its groupings. For the effects of principal succession, see A. Hargreaves & D. Fink (2003), Sustaining leadership, *Phi Delta Kappan*, 84(9), 693–700; see also D. Fink and C. Brayman (2004), Principals' succession and educational change, *Journal of Educational Administration*, 42(4), 431–449. I also address this issue in Chapter Four.

32. J. Ryan, Educational administrators' perceptions of racism in diverse school contexts, *Race, Ethnicity and Education*, 6(2), (2003b), 145–164.

33. There are exceptions, though; see Blase & Anderson (1995).

34. J. Blase & J. Blase (2000), Principals' perspectives on shared governance leadership, *Journal of School Leadership*, 10(1), 9–39.

35. M. Smylie, S. Conley, & H. Marks (2002), Building leadership into the roles of teachers, in J. Murphy (Ed.), *The educational leadership challenge: Redefining leadership for the 21st century* (Chicago: National Society for the Study of Education), 162–188.

36. For a thorough review, see M. Smylie (1997), Research on teacher leadership: Assessing the state of the art, in B. Biddle, T. Good, & I. Goodson (Eds.), *International handbook of teachers and teaching* (Dordrecht, Netherlands: Kluwer), 521–592.

37. S. Bacharach, P. Bamberger, S. Conley & S. Bauer (1990), The dimensionality of decision participation in educational organizations: The value of a multi-domain evaluative approach, *Educational Administration Quarterly*, 26(2), 126–167; A. Somech (2002), Explicating the complexity of participative management: An investigation of multiple dimensions, *Educational Administration Quarterly*, 38(3), 341–371; Smylie (1997).

38. P. Short & J. Rinehart (1992), School Participant Empowerment Scale: Assessment of level of empowerment within the school environment, *Educational and Psychological Measurement*, 52, 951–960.

39. P. Kirby (1992), Shared decision making: Moving from concerns about restrooms to concerns about classrooms, *Journal of School Leadership*, 2(3), 330–345.

40. K. Leithwood, D. Jantzi, & R. Steinbach (1999a), Changing leadership: A menu of possibilities, in *Changing leadership for changing times* (Buckingham, U.K.: Open University Press).

41. Leithwood, Jantzi, & Steinbach (1999a).

42. Smylie, Conley, & Marks (2002).

43. Leithwood, Jantzi, & Steinbach, (1999a).

44. Smylie (1997).

45. Smylie (1997).

46. J. Blase & J. Blase (1997), *The fire is back? Principals sharing school governance* (Thousand Oaks, CA: Corwin).

47. M. Imber & D. Duke (1984), Teacher participation in school decision making: A framework for research, *The Journal of Educational Administration, 22*(1), 24–34.

48. J. Blase & S. Dungan (1994), Tabla rasa: Case studies of shared governance, *School Organization, 14*(2), 209–218.; J. Epp & C. MacNeil (1997), Perceptions of shared governance in an elementary school, *Canadian Journal of Education 22*(3), 254–267; Kirby (1992); P. Short & J. Greer (1997), *Leadership in empowered schools: Themes from innovative efforts.* (Columbus, OH: Merrill).

49. Somech (2002); for other continua, see Short & Greer (1997) and V. Crockenberg & W. Clark (1979), Teacher participation in school decision making: The San Jose Teacher Involvement Project, *Phi Delta Kappan, 61*(2), 115–118.

50. R. Barth (2001), Teacher leader, *Phi Delta Kappan, 82*(6), 443–449; P. Bredeson (1989), Redefining leadership and the roles of school principals: Responses to changes in the professional worklife of teachers, *High School Journal, 73*, 9–20; S. Conley (1991), Review of research on teacher participation in school decision making, in G. Grant (Ed.), *Review of Research in Education* (Washington, DC: American Educational Research Association), 225–265; Crockenberg & Clark (1979); D. Duke, B. Showers, & M. Imber (1980), Teachers and shared decision making: The costs and benefits of involvement, *Educational Administration Quarterly, 16*(1), 93–106; P. Goldman, D. Dunlap, & D. Conley (1993), Facilitative power and nonstandardized solutions to school site restructuring, *Educational Administration Quarterly, 29*(1), 69–92; Imber & Duke (1984); J. Rinehart, P. Short, R. Short, & M. Eckley (1998), Teacher empowerment and principal leadership: Understanding

the influence process, *Educational Administration Quarterly, 34,* 630–649; Short & Greer (1997); Somech (2002).

51. Imber & Duke (1984).

52. J. Epp & C. MacNeil (1997), Perceptions of shared governance in an elementary school, *Canadian Journal of Education, 22*(3), 254–267.; J. Blase & J. Blase (1999), Principals' instructional development and teacher development: Teachers' perspectives, *Educational Administration Quarterly, 38*(3), 349–378.

53. Barth (2001).

54. Somech (2002).

55. M. Wallace (2001), Sharing leadership of schools through teamwork: A justifiable risk? *Educational Management and Administration, 29*(2), 153–168.

56. F. Bolin (1989), Empowering leadership, *Teachers College Record 91*(1), 81–96.

57. Blase & Blase (1997); Blase & Dungan (1994); Bredeson (1989); C. Frost, J. Wakely, & R. Ruh (1974), *The Scanlon plan for organizational development: Identity, participation and equity* (East Lansing: Michigan State University); C. Glickman, L. Allen, & B. Lunsford (1994), Voices of principals from democratically transformed schools, in J. Murphy & K. S. Louis (Eds.), *Reshaping the Principalship: Insights from Transformational Reform Efforts* (Thousand Oaks, CA: Corwin), 203–218; S. Keith & R. Girling (1991), *Education, management and participation* (Toronto: Allyn & Bacon); Leithwood, Jantzi, & Steinbach (1999a); K. Leithwood & D. Jantzi (2000), The effects of different sources of leadership on student engagement in school, in K. Riley & K. S. Louis (Eds.), *Leadership for change and school reform: International perspectives* (New York: Routledge/Falmer Press), 50–66; B. Lunsford (1995), A league of our own, *Educational Leadership, 52*(7), 59–61; Smylie (1997); Smylie, Conley, & Marks (2002).

58. Blase & Blase (1997); Blase & Dungan (1994); Bredeson (1989); J. Rinehart, P. Short, R. Short, & M. Eckley (1997), Teacher

empowerment and teacher leadership: Understanding the influence process, *Educational Administration Quarterly, 34*(4), 630–649;
Smylie (1997).

59. Blase & Blase (1997); Blase & Dungan (1994); Conley (1991);
Epp & MacNeil (1997); Frost, Wakely, & Ruh (1974); Keith &
Girling (1991); Kirby (1992); E. Rice & G. Schneider (1994), A
decade of teacher empowerment: An empirical analysis of teacher
involvement in decision-making, 1980–1991, *Journal of Educational
Administration, 32*(1), 43–58; P. Short & J. Rinehart (1992),
School participant empowerment scale: Assessment of level of
empowerment within the school environment, *Educational and
Psychological Measurement, 52,* 951–960; ; Smylie (1997).

60. Blase & Blase (1997); Rinehart, Short, Short, & Eckley (1997);
Smylie (1997).

61. Kirby (1992).

62. Blase & Blase (1997); Blase & Blase (1999); Bolin (1989); Kirby
(1992).

63. Bolin, (1989); Bredeson (1989); Wallace (2001).

64. Epp & MacNeil (1997); Blase and Blase (1999).

65. Conley (1991); A. Datnow & M. Castellano (2001), Managing
and guiding school reform: Leadership in Success for All schools,
Educational Administration Quarterly, 37(2), 219–249; Duke,
Showers, & Imber (1980).

66. Blase & Blase (1997); Bredeson (1989); R. Clift, M. Johnson,
P. Holland, & M. Veal (1992), Developing the potential for collaborative school leadership, *American Educational Research Journal,
20*(4), 877–908; Datnow & Castellano (2001); Epp & MacNeil
(1997); Leithwood, Jantzi, & Steinbach, (1999a).

67. Blase & Blase (1997); Blase & Blase (1999); Clift, Johnson,
Holland, & Veal (1992); Glickman, Allen, & Lunsford (1994);
M Smylie & J. Brownlea-Conyers (1992), Teacher leaders and
their principals: Exploring the development of new working relationships, *Educational Administration Quarterly 28*(2), 150–184.

68. Blase & Blase (1997); Glickman, Allen, & Lunsford (1994).

69. Blase & Blase (1999); Bredeson (1989); Clift, Johnson, Holland, & Veal (1992); Conley (1991); Duke, Showers, & Imber (1980); Epp & MacNeil (1997); Short & Greer (1997).

70. Conley (1991).

71. K. Leithwood, R. Steinbach, & D. Jantzi (2002), School leadership and teachers' motivation to implement accountability policies, *Educational Administration Quarterly, 38*(1), 94–119.

72. Blase & Dungan (1994); Epp & MacNeil (1997); Kirby (1992); Short & Greer (1997).

73. Blase & Blase (1997); Blase & Blase (1999); Bredeson (1989); Epp & MacNeil (1997).

74. Blase & Blase (2000).

75. Blase & Blase (1997); Blase & Blase (2000).

76. Datnow & Castellano (2001).

77. Short & Greer (1997).

78. Blase & Blase (1997); Blase & Blase (1999); Datnow & Castellano (2001); Epp & MacNeil (1997); Glickman, Allen, & Lunsford (1994); Short & Greer (1997).

79. Bredeson (1989).

80. Datnow & Castellano (2001); Short & Greer (1997).

81. Crockenberg & Clark (1979).

82. Blase & Blase (2000); Crockenberg & Clark (1979).

83. Duke, Showers, & Imber (1980); Short & Greer (1997).

84. Crockenberg & Clark (1979); Epp & MacNeil (1997); Short & Greer (1997).

85. Leithwood, Jantzi, & Steinbach (1999a).

86. Datnow & Castellano (2001); Short & Greer (1997).

87. Short & Greer (1997).

88. Blase & Blase (1997); Bredeson (1989); Short & Greer (1997).

89. Blase & Blase, (1999); Short & Greer (1997).

90. Short & Greer (1997).

91. Bolin (1989); Goldman, Dunlap, & Conley (1993); Short & Greer (1997).

92. Blase & Blase (1999); Blase & Blase (2000).

93. Blase & Blase (1999).

94. Goldman, Dunlap, & Conley (1993); Short & Greer (1997).

95. Goldman, Dunlap, & Conley (1993).

96. Blase & Blase (1999); Blase & Blase (2000); Clift, Johnson, Holland, & Veal (1992); J. Keedy & A. Finch (1994), Examining teacher-principal empowerment: An analysis of power, *Journal of Research and Development in Education* 27(3), 162–175.

97. Blase & Blase (2000).

98. Blase & Blase (2000); Clift, Johnson, Holland, & Veal (1992); Keedy & Finch (1994).

99. Clift, Johnson, Holland, & Veal (1992).

100. Blase & Blase (2000); Glickman, Allen, & Lunsford (1994).

101. D. Ross & R. Webb (1995), Implementing shared decision-making at Brooksville Elementary School. In A. Lieberman (Ed.), *The work of restructuring schools: Building from the ground up* (New York: Teachers College Press): 64–86.

102. Ross & Webb (1995), 72–73.

103. Ross & Webb (1995), 77.

104. E. Bondy (1995), Fredericks Middle School and the dynamics of school reform, in A. Lieberman (Ed.), *The work of restructuring schools: Building from the ground up* (New York: Teachers College Press, 1995): 43–63.

105. Bondy (1995), 57.

106. P. Gronn (2002), Distributed leadership, in K. Leithwood & P. Hallinger (Eds.), *The second international handbook of educational leadership and administration* (Dordrecht, Netherlands: Kluwer), 653–696; Smylie, Conley, & Marks (2002).

107. Of course, this is not new. A recognition of the importance of context goes back at least to the 1950s. See, for example, F. Fiedler (1967), *A theory of leadership effectiveness* (New York: McGraw-Hill).

108. Gronn (2002); D. Pounder, R. Ogawa, & E. Adams (1995), Leadership as an organization-wide phenomenon: Its impact on school performance, *Educational Administration Quarterly, 31*(4), 564–588; J. Spillane, R. Halverson, & J. Diamond (2001), Investigating school leadership practice: A distributed perspective, *Educational Researcher, 30*(3), 23–28.

109. Leithwood, Jantzi, & Steinbach, (1999a); Smylie, Conley, & Marks (2002).

110. Blase & Blase (1999); Blase & Dungan (1994); S. Critchley (2003), The nature and extent of student involvement in educational policy-making in Canadian school systems, *Educational Management and Administration 31*(1), 97–106; B. Levin (2001), Putting students at the centre of educational reform, *Journal of Educational Change, 1*(2), 155–172; B. Levin (1998), The educational requirement for democracy, *Curriculum Inquiry 28*(1), 57–79; Short & Greer (1997).

111. Critchley (2003).

112. D. Bechtel & C. Reed (1998), Students as documenters: Benefits, reflections and suggestions, *NASSP Bulletin, 82*(594), 89–95; Critchley (2003); Fletcher (1998), Democratization on trial: Democratization in English secondary schools, in K. Jensen and S. Walker (Eds.), *Toward democratic schooling: European experiences* (Philadelphia: Open University Press); W. Furtwengler (1996), Improving secondary school discipline by involving students in the process, *NASSP Bulletin, 80*(581), 36–44; Levin (1998); J. Young & B. Levin (1998), *Understanding Canadian schools: An introduction to educational administration* (Toronto: Harcourt Brace).

113. Critchley (2003).

114. Levin (1998).

115. C. Lindeman (2004), *Participatory governance: The role of student trustees on Ontario school boards*, unpublished doctoral dissertation, University of Toronto.

116. E. Wood (1977), *Student influence in decision making in secondary schools,* unpublished doctoral dissertation, University of Toronto.

117. A. Osler & H. Starkey (1998), Children's rights and citizenship: Some implications for the management of schools, *International Journal of Children's Rights,* 6, 313–333; Critchley (2003); Wood (1977).

118. Osler & Starkey (1998).

119. Levin (2001); Furtwengler (1996).

120. Levin (2001); Levin (1998); E. Weber (1996), Creating communities in high school: An interactive learning and training approach, *NASSP Bulletin,* 80(583), 76–85.

121. A. Kohn (1999), *The schools our children deserve* (New York: Houghton Mifflin); Levin (2001).

122. Levin (1998); J. Scane & R. Wignall (1996), Students in school councils: The clients speak, *Orbit,* 27(4), 13–14; D. Treslan (1983), A mechanism for involving students in decision making: A critical issue in educational planning and administration, *Clearing House,* 57(3), 124–131.

123. See, for example, R. Mackin (1996), Hey Bob, Can we talk? Toward the creation of a personalized high school, *NASSP Bulletin,* 80(584), 9–16; L. Lee & S. Ursel (2001), Individual learning, school environment, secondary schools, *Education Canada,* 40(4), 12–13; Leisey and others (1997) in S. Critchley (1999), *The nature and extent of student involvement in educational policy-making in Canadian school systems,* doctoral dissertation, University of Toronto; B. Trafford (1997), *Participation, power sharing and school improvement* (Nottingham, U.K.: Educational Heretics Press).

124. Furtwengler (1996).

125. J. Hirata (2003), *Do school councils empower students? Two Japanese case studies.* Unpublished doctoral dissertation, University of Toronto.

126. Hirata (2003), 114.

127. A. Hargreaves, L. Earl, S. Moore, & S. Manning (2001), *Learning to change: Teaching beyond subjects and standards* (San Francisco: Jossey-Bass).

128. Hargreaves, Earl, Moore, & Manning (2001), 40–41.

129. Hargreaves, Earl, Moore, & Manning (2001), 71.

130. Levin (2001); Levin (1998).

131. See, for example, J. Epstein (1997), *School, family and community partnerships: Your handbook for action* (Thousand Oaks, CA: Corwin Press); K. Leithwood, D. Jantzi & R. Steinbach (1999b), Do school councils matter? *Educational Policy, 13*(4), 467–493.

132. D. Lewis & K. Nakagawa (1995), *Race and educational reform in the American metropolis: A study of school decentralization* (Albany: State University of New York Press).

133. See, for example, S. Carmichael & C. Hamilton (1967), *Black power: The politics of liberation in America.* (New York: Random House); M. Fine (1993), [Ap]parent involvement: Reflections on parents, power, and urban public schools, *Teachers College Record* 94(4), 682–710; H. Levin (Ed.) (1970), *Community control of schools* (New York: Clarion).

134. Lewis & Nakagawa (1995).

135. See, for example, J. Comer (1986), Parent participation in the schools, *Phi Delta Kappan, 67*(6), 442–446; Epstein (1997); S. Lawrence-Lightfoot (1978), *Worlds apart: Relationships between families and schools* (New York: Basic Books).

136. Lewis & Nakagawa (1995).

137. Fine (1993); Lewis & Nakagawa (1995).

138. See, for example, M. Apple (2000), Racing toward educational reform, in R. Mahalingam & C. McCarthy (Eds.), *Multicultural curriculum* (New York: Routledge), 84–107; R. Hatcher, B. Troyna, & D. Gewirtz (1996), *Racial equality and the local management of schools* (Stattfordshire, U.K.: Trentham Books); Leithwood, Jantzi & Steinbach, (1999b).

139. Lewis & Nakagawa (1995).

140. Leithwood, Jantzi & Steinbach (1999b).

141. Hatcher, Troyna, & Gewirtz (1996).

142. Lewis & Nakagawa (1995).

143. G. Hess (1999), Expectations, opportunity, capacity and will: The four essential components of Chicago school reform, *Educational Policy, 13*(4), 494–517; D. Shipps, J. Kahne, & M. Smylie (1999), The politics of urban school reform: Legitimacy, city growth and school improvement in Chicago, *Educational Policy, 13*(4), 518–545.

144. P. Chambers (2001), *Ontario school councils: Engaging diversity,* unpublished master's research project, University of Toronto; C. Delgado-Gaitan (1991), Involving parents in schools: A process of empowerment, *American Journal of Education, 100*(1), 20–46; K. Delhi (1994), *Parent activism and school reform in Toronto: A report* (Toronto: Department of Sociology in Education, Ontario Institute for Studies in Education); Hatcher, Troyna, & Gewirtz (1996).

145. Hatcher, Troyna, & Gewirtz (1996).

146. Delhi (1994); Hatcher, Troyna, & Gewirtz (1996).

147. Lewis & Nakagawa (1995).

148. Hatcher, Troyna, & Gewirtz (1996).

149. Fine (1993), 696.

150. Delhi (1994); G. Hess (1995), *Restructuring urban schools: A Chicago perspective* (New York: Teachers College Press); Leithwood, Jantzi & Steinbach (1999b); B. Malen & R. Ogawa (1992), Community involvement: Parents, teachers and administrators working together, in S. Bacharach (Ed.), *Education reform: Making sense of it all* (Toronto: Allyn & Bacon), 103–119.

151. E. Odden & P. Wohlsletter (1995), Making school-based management work, *Educational Leadership 52*(5), 32–36.

152. Of course, in situations where councils have the power to dismiss principals, the relationship between council and principal may be

different, even though principals still would have access to resources that council members do not.

153. G. Dei & I. James (2002), Beyond the rhetoric: Moving from exclusion, reaching for inclusion in Canadian schools, *Alberta Journal of Educational Research, 48*(1), 77.

154. B. Peterson (1999), La Escuela Fratney: A journey towards democracy, in M. Apple & J. Beane (Eds.), *Democratic schools: Lessons from the chalk face* (Buckingham, U.K.: Open University Press), 68–97.

155. Hess (1999); Shipps, Kahne, & Smylie (1999).

156. Oakes, J., & Lipton, M. (2002), Struggling for educational equity in diverse communities: School reform as social movement, *Journal of Educational Change, 3*(4), 383–406.

157. Fine (1993).

158. Lewis & Nakagawa (1995).

159. Oakes & Lipton (2002).

160. Shipps, Kahne, & Smylie (1999).

161. R. Thomas with S. Macanawai & C. MacLaurin (1997), Editorial, *Journal of Educational Administration, 35*(5), 385–396.

162. Thomas, Macanawai, & MacLaurin (1997); J. Bailey & D. du Plessis (1997), Understanding principals' attitudes toward inclusive schooling, *Journal of Educational Administration, 35*(5), 428–438.

163. Thomas, Macanawai, & MacLaurin (1997); Bailey & du Plessis (1997).

164. Bailey & du Plessis (1997).

165. L. Doyle (2002), Leadership and inclusion: Reculturing for reform, *International Journal of Educational Reform 11*(1), 38–62; P. Ingram (1997), Leadership behaviours of principals in inclusive educational settings, *Journal of Educational Administration, 35*(5), 411–427; Bailey & du Plessis (1997); M. Keys, C. Hanley-Maxwell, & C. Capper (1999), Spirituality? It's the core of my leadership: Empowering leadership in an inclusive elementary school, *Educational Administration Quarterly 35*(2), 203–237; N. Guzman (1997),

Leadership for successful inclusive schools: A study of principal behaviours, *Journal of Educational Administration* 35(5), 439–450; Thomas, Macanawai, & MacLaurin (1997).

166. Ingram (1997); D. Mayrowetz & C. Weinstein (1999), Sources of leadership for inclusive education: Creating schools for all children, *Educational Administration Quarterly*, 35(3), 423–449; Thomas, Macanawai, & MacLaurin (1997).

167. Ingram (1997).

168. Bailey & du Plessis (1997).

169. C. Boucher (1981), Teachers' decisions about mainstreaming, *Education Unlimited*, 3(1), 9–11; Ingram (1997); T. Rizzo (1984), Attitudes of physical educators toward handicapped students, *Adapted Physical Activity Quarterly*, 1(4), 267–275.

170. Bailey & du Plessis (1997); Ingram (1997).

171. Bailey & du Plessis (1997); Doyle (2002).

172. Bailey & du Plessis (1997).

173. Doyle (2002); Guzman (1997).

174. See, for example, Ingram (1997).

175. Ingram (1997).

176. See, for example, Doyle (2002).

177. Keys, Hanley-Maxwell, & Capper (1999).

178. J. Thousand & R. Villa (1994), Managing complex change toward inclusive schooling, in R. Villa & J. Thousand (Eds.), *Creating an inclusive school* (Alexandria: VA: Association for Supervision and Curriculum Development), 51–79.

179. Thousand & Villa (1994).

180. Thousand & Villa (1994).

181. Doyle (2002); Keys, Hanley-Maxwell, & Capper, (1999); Mayrowetz & Weinstein (1999); Thousand & Villa (1994).

182. Thousand & Villa (1994).

183. Keys, Hanley-Maxwell, & Capper (1999).

184. Guzman (1997).

185. Mayrowetz & Weinstein (1999).

186. Keys, Hanley-Maxwell, & Capper (1999).

187. Keys, Hanley-Maxwell, & Capper (1999), 217.

188. Keys, Hanley-Maxwell, & Capper (1999), 219.

189. Keys, Hanley-Maxwell, & Capper (1999), 226.

Chapter Four

1. Principals, for example, have only a comparatively small and indirect impact on what happens in their respective organizations. See, for example, P. Hallinger & R. Heck (1998), Exploring the principal's contribution to school effectiveness: 1980–1995, *School Effectiveness and School Improvement, 9*(2), 157–191.

2. Hierarchy may undermine motivation, creativity, and productivity and generate negative consequences for self-concept, task-related and verbal behavior, and willingness to assume responsibility on the part of those in lower positions. See, for example, V. J. Vanderslice (1988), Separating leadership from leaders: An assessment of the effect of leader and follower roles, *Human Relations, 41*(9), 677–696.

3. J. Spillane, R. Halverson, & J. Diamond (2001), Investigating school leadership practice: A distributed perspective, *Educational Researcher, 30*(3), 23–28; D. Pounder, R. Ogawa, & E. Adams (1995), Leadership as an organization-wide phenomenon: Its impact on school performance, *Educational Administration Quarterly, 31*(4), 564–588; P. Gronn (2002), Distributed leadership, in K. Leithwood & P. Hallinger (Eds.), *Second international handbook of educational leadership and administration* (Dordrecht, Netherlands: Kluwer), 653–696; M. Smylie, S. Conley, & H. Marks (2002), Building leadership into the roles of teachers, in J. Murphy (Ed.), *The educational leadership challenge: Redefining leadership for the 21st century* (Chicago: National Society for the Study of Education), 162–188.

4. Spillane, Halverson, & Diamond (2001).

5. Smylie, Conley, & Marks (2002).

6. A. Hargreaves & D. Fink (2003), Sustaining leadership, *Phi Delta Kappan*, 84(9), 693–700; see also D. Fink & C. Brayman (2004), Principals' succession and educational change, *Journal of Educational Administration*, 42(4), 431–449.

7. J. Bailey & D. du Plessis (1997), Understanding principals' attitudes toward inclusive schooling, *Journal of Educational Administration*, 35(5), 428–438; L. Doyle (2002), Leadership and inclusion: Reculturing for reform, *International Journal of Educational Reform*, 11(1), 38–62; P. Ingram (1997), Leadership behaviours of principals in inclusive educational settings, *Journal of Educational Administration*, 35(5), 411–427; D. Mayrowetz & C. Weinstein (1999), Sources of leadership for inclusive education: Creating schools for all children, *Educational Administration Quarterly*, 35(3), 423–449.

8. J. Ryan (2003b), Educational administrators' perceptions of racism in diverse school contexts, *Race, Ethnicity and Education*, 6(2), 145–164; A. Datnow (1998), *The gender politics of educational change* (London: Falmer Press).

9. J. Thousand & R. Villa (1994), Managing complex change toward inclusive schooling, in R. Villa & J. Thousand (Eds.), *Creating an inclusive school* (Alexandria, VA.: Association for Supervision and Curriculum Development), 51–79.

10. Doyle (2002); M. Keys, C. Hanley-Maxwell, & C. Capper (1999), Spirituality? It's the core of my leadership: Empowering leadership in an inclusive elementary school, *Educational Administration Quarterly*, 35(2), 203–237; Mayrowetz & Weinstein (1999); Thousand & Villa (1994).

11. Keys, Hanley-Maxwell, & Capper (1999).

12. Keys, Hanley-Maxwell, & Capper (1999).

13. It is not necessarily the principal's view but the value of inclusion that is important here. Nevertheless, there is a paradox; inclusion is promoted through exclusive means. But this practice may be necessary if including exclusive practices will end up generating more exclusion. At the end of the day, what matters most is the

extent of inclusion. So if promoting these ends requires excluding exclusion, then so be it.

14. Thousand & Villa (1994).

15. Thousand & Villa (1994).

16. T. Gale & K. Densmore (2003), Democratic educational leadership in contemporary times, *International Journal of Leadership in Education*, 6(2), 119–136.

17. Gale & Densmore (2003).

18. J. Oakes & M. Lipton (2002), Struggling for educational equity in diverse communities: School reform as social movement, *Journal of Educational Change*, 3(4), 383–406.

19. Oakes & Lipton (2002).

20. Thousand & Villa (1994).

21. Thousand & Villa (1994).

22. S. May (1994), *Making multicultural education work* (Clevedon, U.K.: Multilingual Matters), 67.

23. J. Ryan (2003a), *Leading diverse schools* (Dordrecht, Netherlands: Kluwer).

24. J. Finkel & G. Bolin (1996), Linking racial identity theory to integrating the curriculum, *College Teaching*, 44(1), 34–36; L. Robertson (1998), *Educators' responses to equity in-service*, unpublished doctoral dissertation, University of Toronto; C. Sleeter (1993), How white teachers construct race, in C. McCarthy & W. Crichlow (Eds.), *Race, identity and representation in education* (New York: Routledge), 157–171.

25. Ryan (2003a).

26. V. A. Herrity & N. S. Glasman (1999), Training administrators for culturally and linguistically diverse school populations: Opinions of expert practitioners, *Journal of School Leadership*, 9, 235–253.

27. P. Goldman, D. Dunlap, & D. Conley (1993), Facilitative power and nonstandardized solutions to school site restructuring, *Educational Administration Quarterly* 29(1), 69–92.

28. Ryan (2003a).

29. G. Griffin (1987), The school in society and the social organization of the school: Social implications for staff development, in M. Wideen & I. Andrews (Eds.), *Staff development for school improvement* (Toronto: Lorimer), 19–37; Robertson (1998).

30. Sleeter (1993).

31. Robertson (1998).

32. See D. Gillborn (1995), *Racism and antiracism in real schools* (Philadelphia: Open University Press).

33. Gillborn (1995), 112.

34. See, for example, K. Leithwood (Ed.) (2000), *Understanding schools as intelligent systems* (Stamford, CT: JAI Press); K. Leithwood & D. Jantzi (2000), The effects of different sources of leadership on student engagement in school, in K. Riley & K. S. Louis (Eds.), *Leadership for change and school reform: International perspectives* (New York: Routledge/Falmer Press), 50–66; K. Leithwood & K. S. Louis (Eds.) (1998), *Organizational learning in schools* (Lisse, Netherlands: Swets & Zeitlinger); P. Senge (1990), *The fifth discipline: The art and practice of the learning organization* (Toronto: Doubleday); P. Senge, N. Cambron-McCabe, T. Lucas, B. Smith, J. Dutton, & A. Kleiner (2000), *Schools that learn* (Toronto: Doubleday).

35. C. Giles & A. Hargreaves (in press), The sustainability of innovative schools as learning organizations and professional learning communities during standardized reform, *Educational Administration Quarterly.*

36. Giles & Hargreaves (in press).

37. C. Larson & C. Ovando (2001), *The color of bureaucracy: The politics of equity in multicultural school communities* (Toronto: Wadsworth); C. Shields (2002, October), *Towards a dialogic approach to understanding values,* paper presented at the 7th annual conference of the Centre for Values and Leadership, Toronto; Sleeter (1993).

38. C. Coombs (2002), *Reflective practice: Developing habits of mind*, unpublished doctoral dissertation, University of Toronto.

39. D. Schön (1983), *The reflective practitioner: How professionals think in action* (New York: Basic Books).

40. N. Burbules & R. Berk (1999), Critical thinking and critical pedagogy: Relations, differences and limits, in T. Popkewitz & L. Fendler (Eds.), *Changing terrains of knowledge and politics* (New York: Routledge), 45–66.

41. Ryan (2003a), 149.

42. Coombs (2002).

43. E. Shohat & R. Stam (1994), *Unthinking Eurocentrism: Multiculturalism and the media* (New York: Routledge).

44. J. Ryan (1994), Transcending the limitations of social science: Insight, understanding and the humanities in educational administration, *Journal of Educational Thought, 28*(3), 225–244.

45. R. Bates (1980), Educational administration, the sociology of science, and the management of knowledge, *Educational Administration Quarterly 16*(2), 1–20.

46. J. Smyth (1996), The socially just alternative to the "self-managing school," in K. Leithwood, J. Chapman, D. Corson, P. Hallinger, & A. Hart (Eds.), *International handbook of educational leadership and administration* (Dordrecht, Netherlands: Kluwer), 1097–1131.

47. B. Peterson (1999), La Escuela Fratney: A journey towards democracy, in M. Apple & J. Beane (Eds.), *Democratic schools: Lessons from the chalk face* (Buckingham, U.K.: Open University Press), 68–97.

48. P. Lipman (1998), *Race, class, and power in school restructuring* (Albany: State University of New York Press); S. Maxcy (1998), Preparing school principals for ethno-democratic leadership, *International Journal of Leadership in Education, 1*(3), 217–235; May (1994); J. Smyth (1998), A "pedagogical" and "educative" view of leadership, in J. Smyth (Ed.), *Critical perspectives on educational leadership* (London: Falmer Press), 179–204.

49. N. Burbules (1993), *Dialogue in teaching: Theory and practice* (New York: Teachers College Press).

50. Burbules (1993).

51. See, for example, J. Habermas (1997), *The theory of communicative action* (Boston: Beacon Press).

52. S. Drake & J. Ryan (1994), Narrative and knowledge: Inclusive pedagogy for contemporary times, *Curriculum and Teaching*, 9(1), 45–56.

53. C. Levine-Rasky (1993, June), *Listening as an appropriate response by members of privileged groups*. Paper presented at the meeting of the Canadian Society for the Study of Education, Carleton University, Ottawa.

54. L. Delpit (1988), The silenced dialogue: Power and pedagogy in educating other people's children, *Harvard Educational Review*, 5(8), 297.

55. E. Ellsworth (1989), Why doesn't this feel empowering? Working through the repressive myths of critical pedagogy, *Harvard Educational Review*, 9(3), 297–324.

56. Ellsworth (1989).

57. G. Hess (1999), Expectations, opportunity, capacity and will: The four essential components of Chicago school reform, *Educational Policy*, 13(4), 494–517; D. Shipps, J. Kahne, & M. Smylie (1999), The politics of urban school reform: Legitimacy, city growth and school improvement in Chicago, *Educational Policy*, 13(4), 518–545.

58. C. Riehl (2000), The principal's role in creating inclusive schools for diverse students: A review of normative, empirical, and critical literature on the practice of educational administration, *Review of Educational Research*, 70(1), 55–82.

59. J. Blase & J. Blase (1999), Implementation of shared governance for instructional improvement: Principals' perspectives, *Journal of Educational Administration*, 37(5), 476–500.

60. D. Waite (1995), *Rethinking instructional supervision: Notes on language and culture* (London: Falmer Press); D. Waite & M. R. Fernandes (2000), Complicity in supervision: Another

postmodern moment, in J. Glantz & L. Behar-Horenstein (Eds.), *Paradigm debates in curriculum and supervision: Modern and postmodern perspectives* (Westport, CT: Bergin & Garvey), 190–211.

61. Blase & Blase (1999).

62. Blase & Blase (1999).

63. Blase & Blase (1999).

64. P. Kleine-Kracht (1993), Indirect instructional leadership: An administrator's choice, *Educational Administrative Quarterly, 29*(2), 187–211.

65. Kleine-Kracht (1993).

66. B. Joyce & B. Showers (1995), *Student achievement through staff development* (New York: Longman).

67. Kleine-Kracht (1993).

68. Kleine-Kracht (1993), 201.

69. A. Lieberman & L. Miller (2004), *Teacher leadership* (San Francisco: Jossey-Bass).

70. R. Simon (1992), *Teaching against the grain: Texts for a pedagogy of possibility* (Toronto: OISE).

71. See, for example, L. McNeil (2000), *Contradictions of school reform: Educational costs of standardized testing* (New York: Routledge).

72. S. Krug (1992), Instructional leadership: A constructivist perspective, *Educational Administration Quarterly, 28*(3), 430–443.

73. J. Cummins (1986), Empowering minority students: A framework for intervention, *Harvard Educational Review, 56*(1), 18–36.

74. M. Fine (1993), [Ap]parent involvement: Reflections on parents, power, and urban public schools, *Teachers College Record, 94*(4), 682–710; R. Hatcher, B. Troyna, & D. Gewirtz (1996), *Racial equality and the local management of schools* (Stattfordshire, U.K.: Trentham Books); D. Lewis & K. Nakagawa (1995), *Race and educational reform in the American metropolis: A study of school decentralization* (Albany: State University of New York Press); Ryan (2003a).

75. D. Corson (1996b), Critical policy making: Emancipatory school-site leadership in multi-ethnic schools, *Forum of Education*, *52*(2).

76. May (1994).

77. Ryan (2003a).

78. See, for example, Gillborn (1995).

79. Corson (1996b).

80. K. Delhi (1994), *Parent activism and school reform in Toronto: A report* (Toronto: Department of Sociology in Education, Ontario Institute for Studies in Education); K. Leithwood, D. Jantzi, & R. Steinbach (1999a), Changing leadership: A menu of possibilities, in *Changing leadership for changing times* (Buckingham, U.K.: Open University Press); B. Malen & R. Ogawa (1992), Community involvement: Parents, teachers and administrators working together, in S. Bacharach (Ed.), *Education reform: Making sense of it all* (Toronto: Allyn & Bacon), 103–119.

81. Corson (1996b).

82. Gillborn (1995).

83. May (1994).

84. Gillborn (1995).

85. See, for example, T. Peters & R. Waterman (1982), *In search of excellence* (New York: Harper).

86. U. Reitzug & J. Reeves (1992), Miss Lincoln doesn't teach here anymore: A descriptive narrative and conceptual analysis of a principal's symbolic leadership behavior, *Educational Administration Quarterly*, *28*(2), 185–219.

87. T. Deal & K. Peterson (1994), *The leadership paradox: Balancing logic and artistry in schools* (San Francisco: Jossey-Bass).

88. See, for example, L. Angus (1996), Cultural dynamics and organizational analysis: Leadership, administration and the management of meaning in school, in K. Leithwood, J. Chapman, D. Corson, P. Hallinger, & A. Hart (Eds.), *International handbook of educational leadership and administration* (Dordrecht, Netherlands: Kluwer),

967–998; R. Bates (1987), Corporate culture, schooling and educational administration, *Educational Administration Quarterly, 23*(4), 79–115.

89. Bates (1987).

90. G. Anderson (1990), Toward a critical constructivist approach to school administration: Invisibility, legitimation, and the study of non-events, *Educational Administration Quarterly, 26*(1), 38–59.

91. Gillborn (1995).

Index

TITLES IN THE JOSSEY-BASS
LEADERSHIP LIBRARY IN EDUCATION SERIES

Ann Lieberman, Lynne Miller
Teacher Leadership

Teacher Leadership is written for teachers who assume responsibility for educational success beyond their own classrooms by providing peer support, modeling good practice, or coordinating curriculum and instruction. It offers cases studies of innovative programs and stories of individual teachers who lead in a variety of contexts. It shows how to develop learning communities that include rather than exclude, create knowledge rather than merely applying it, and provide challenge and support to new and experienced teachers.

ISBN 0-7879-6245-7   Paperback   112 Pages   2004

Robert J. Starratt
Ethical Leadership

In *Ethical Leadership*, Robert Starratt—one of the leading thinkers on the topic of ethics and education—shows educational leaders how to move beyond mere technical efficiency in the delivery and performance of learning. He explains that leadership requires a moral commitment to high quality learning, based on three essential virtues: proactive responsibility, personal and professional authenticity, and an affirming, critical, and enabling presence.

ISBN 0-7879-6564-2   Paperback   176 Pages   2004

Andy Hargreaves, Dean Fink
Sustainable Leadership

One of the most important and neglected aspects of leadership is leadership succession. Schools tend to focus on improving schools or remaking them anew rather than sustaining what has been created by past leaders. Similarly, leaders rarely think about how the improvements they make will survive their own departure. In this book, Andy Hargreaves and Dean Fink examine what we know about making leadership last. They offer an overview of the topic, a summary of research, examples of best practices, and guidelines all based on their seven principles of sustainability: depth, length, breadth, justice, diversity, resourcefulness, and conservation.

ISBN 0-7879-6838-2   Paperback   256 Pages   Fall 2005

Michael Fullan
Turnaround Leadership
ISBN 0-7879-6985-0   Paperback   128 Pages (approx.)   Spring 2006

James Spillane
Distributed Leadership
ISBN 0-7879-6538-3   Paperback   112 Pages (approx.)   Spring 2006

Geoffrey Southworth
Learner-Centered Leadership
ISBN 0-7879-7553-2   Paperback   128 Pages (approx.)   Fall 2006